RECIPES *from* CENTRAL MARKET

RECIPES *from* CENTRAL MARKET

Favorite Recipes from the Standholders of the Nation's Oldest Farmers Market, Central Market in Lancaster, Pennsylvania

Phyllis Pellman Good *and* Louise Stoltzfus

Good Books

Intercourse, PA 17534

For all who have given life
to Central Market—
its standholders, its customers,
its advocates throughout the region

Photography by Mark Beach

Design by Dawn J. Ranck

RECIPES FROM CENTRAL MARKET
Copyright © 1996 by Good Books, Intercourse, PA 17534
International Standard Book Number: 1-56148-210-2 (hard)
International Standard Book Number: 1-56148-222-6 (paper)
Library of Congress Card Number: 96-27558

Library of Congress Cataloging-in-Publication Data
Good, Phyllis Pellman
    Recipes from Central Market : favorite recipes from the standholders of the
nation's oldest farmers market, Central Market in Lancaster, Pennsylvania /
Phyllis Pellman Good and Louise Stoltzfus.
        p. cm.
    Includes index.
    ISBN 1-56148-210-2 (hardcover.) -- ISBN 1-56148-222-6 (pbk.)
    1. Cookery. 2. Central Market (Lancaster, Pa.) I. Stoltzfus, Louise.
II. Central Market (Lancaster, Pa.) III. Title.
TX714.G665   1996
641.5--dc20   96-27558
                                                                CIP

Table of Contents

About This Cookbook—
and the Place from Which It Came

There stands, just off the center square in downtown Lancaster, Pennsylvania, a monument to a food and gardening tradition— Central Market—both a building and an event. It is an architectural wonder in its gracefully historic character. It is a throbbing and enduring center, supported by its residential neighbors, the business and professional workers who share its streets, and all the loyals who drive in from greater Lancaster and even nearby states.

What brings the customers? What holds the standholders? What sustains the remarkable life in this place when the city that surrounds it must fend off a slow-down of commercial activity, a dwindling tax base, and fears of crime?

There are answers: Food that can't be resisted because it is carefully grown or produced by knowledgeable hands. Spirited standholders who understand their work as artisans. Devoted customers who know that going to market is always worth the trip, the earlier in the day, the better. A city who recognizes the treasure it has and continually interprets (and re-interprets) the market's charter—and intervenes when it is challenged.

Those who bring their bounty to market, and those who line up to take it away, know good food. They are attuned to the seasons. They understand texture and flavor. They enjoy the robust and the subtle. These "experts"—who work with the basics, the truck-patch-grown, the home-baked, the hand-prepared—have gathered together their own favorite recipes for this cookbook.

Some of these recipes call for products the standholders produce and sell, some are well rooted traditional dishes, some are simply personal favorites. As a collection, *Recipes from Central Market* mirrors the mix that Central Market is—the historic and novel, the foods of the long-settled Germans and the more-recently-arrived Asians and Lebanese, startlingly simple dishes and also multi-stepped productions.

We are grateful to the many standholders who took time away from their market-tending and market preparation to put their recipes in readable form for this book. Market Master Don Horn and fourth-generation standholder Viv Hunt made many connections for us. Joy Kraybill ably oversaw many details. Steve Scott did considerable research on the market's history and wrote much of the historical material. Thank you all.

Central Market offers its pleasure with food when you visit its brick-walled aisles—or when you prepare any of these choice recipes.

—Phyllis Pellman Good and Louise Stoltzfus

Central Market
Lancaster, Pennsylvania

Lancaster's Central Market becomes a vitally active place of commerce and friendship every Tuesday, Friday, and Saturday. Then, with dependable regularity, trucks, vans, and station wagons crowd the streets and alleys surrounding the Romanesque building. Before daybreak, market standholders "set up"—unpacking and displaying their wares that attract a steady stream of customers from far and near.

It is a tradition for standholders and market shoppers alike—"once it's in your blood," they say, "you can't stay away." For what compares with fresh tomatoes and herbs gathered just a few hours earlier, with pecan rolls and cherry crumb pies made only yesterday, with meat prepared in nearby smokehouses, and with seeing friends at least once a week?

Central Market was built in 1889. But the habit of going to market is older still. When Andrew and James Hamilton planned the town in 1730, they provided for a market place, measuring 120 feet square.

When Lancaster was incorporated as a borough in 1742, its charter from George II of England established the market practice: "And we do further grant for us, our heirs and successors . . . to have, hold, and keep . . . two markets in each week." Already in 1744 a visitor in the town remarked, "They have a good market in this town, well filled with provisions of all kinds and prodigiously cheap." A few decades later (in 1776) a British officer paroled in Lancaster remarked, "Food is very plentiful. The markets abound with most excellent cyder and provisions."

The first Lancaster farmers market was held outdoors, but by 1757 a market house had been constructed, although it was probably a rather primitive structure. In 1763 part of the market house was reserved for the storage of three fire engines.

The city was soon under pressure to erect a larger and more substantial building for market. For a while, the farmers market shared a building with City Hall and a Masonic Lodge. Before long, this proved to be an inadequate solution. But a shortage of nearby available property made it nearly impossible to meet the demands of vendors and customers alike.

◆

The Curb Market and Neighborhood Markets

Finally, in the 1820s, in order to relieve the situation, farmers were permitted to back their wagons up to the curbs along the streets and sell their goods directly from their vehicles or temporary stands. This gathering of sellers became known as the curb market. It was an outgrowth of Central Market, but it developed as a distinct entity.

After the First World War, motor vehicles began replacing horse-drawn wagons at the curb market. Eventually, increased auto traffic through the city caused the curb market to be impractical and unsafe. On January 1, 1927, the city decreed that this colorful institution come to an end. The standholders were offered space in the Southern Market.

In the late 1800s, as the city was scrambling to provide adequate space for its marketers, a series of neighborhood markets opened throughout Lancaster. In fact, there were at least eight other farmers markets that once operated within Lancaster. It was not unusual for standholders to sell at several different markets on different days of the week.

These were the markets, their years of operation, and their locations:

• The Curb Market, 1818-1927.

• The Northern Market, 1872-1953, on the northwest corner of Queen and Walnut Streets.

• The Eastern Market, 1882-1918, on the southeast corner of King and Shippen Streets.

• The Western Market, 1882-1920, on the southeast corner of Orange and Pine Streets.

• The Southern Market, 1888-1986, on the southwest corner of Queen and Vine Streets.

• The Fulton Market, 1907-1971, on Plum Street, between Frederick and Hand Streets.

• The Arcade Market, 1927-1965, between Orange and Marion Streets, and between Prince and Market Streets.

• The West End Market, 1954-1985, on the northwest corner of Lemon and Mary Streets.

It was in 1889 that the current Central Market building was erected. Very little change was made to the market house until 1973. Then, as part of an urban renewal project, the city began major restoration work on the structure. Because the market was by then listed on the National Register of Historic Places, the Department of Housing and Urban Development provided a grant of $402,000, and the city supplied matching funds.

Under the direction of architect S. Dale Kaufman, stands were relocated to provide more aisle space, and a new underground electrical system and sewers were installed. Despite considerable inconvenience to the standholders and shoppers, the mayor announced that the market would stay open during the whole renovation process in order to keep a two-century-old tradition alive. The refurbished market house was officially dedicated on March 21, 1975.

Most stalls or units were now six feet long with a few being nine feet or an irregular length. In the new arrangement the stands requiring plumbing facilities for cleanup (fresh meat, fish, etc.) were limited to the rows along three of the walls and rows B and C on the west side.

One long-standing tradition changed in the remodeled market house: the fish stands were relocated inside the building. Previously fish was sold only outside at stands along the north side of the market house. Adequate ventilation in the new Central Market took care of a potential odor problem.

A tiny restaurant that occupied the southeast corner of the market was done away with during the remodeling. City Council wished to retain the *marketplace* character of Central Market, rather than having it become an *eating* place. However, one sandwich stand was permitted, intended mainly for the convenience of the standholders who wished to eat at the market. Many lunchtime shoppers like to buy a small quantity of meat at one stand and a roll at another stand in order to make their own sandwich while at the market.

There is no doubt that Central Market has become one of Lancaster's main attractions. Despite a deluge of out-of-town visitors, City Council has made a concentrated effort to keep the market a true farmers market and not one that views visitors as its primary customers. The regulations specify that the stands "be used solely for the sale of food products and farm produced goods . . ." Several stands established before the ruling went into effect continued to sell craft and souvenir type items. No new stands will be granted this privilege.

Market Auctions and Rents

Standholders pay a yearly rent for the stalls they occupy. When a standholder wants to discontinue business at the market, the vacant stand goes up for public auction. These auctions usually take place in December. The price paid for a stall at the auction serves as the first year's rent for the stand. In addition to people obtaining a stand for the first time, some market stalls are sold to those already having

◆

stands who wish to expand their businesses or move to a better position. Normally, one party is allowed to own no more than four stands at the market.

A market regulation specifies that a vacant stand first be offered for lease "for the same general type of use for which it was used immediately prior to the auction." If no one bids under this provision, then the stand may be open to bidders wishing to use it for other purposes.

When a standholder dies, the market stand may be passed to a spouse or child without being resold at auction. Several market stands are currently occupied by descendants of families who have had stands for three, four, and even five generations.

The Market Master

In the wee hours of every Tuesday, Friday, and Saturday morning a lone man's footsteps echo down the brick sidewalks to the Central Market house. He goes to the various entrances, unlocking the large metal doors, just ahead of the trucks bringing fruits, vegetables, meat, fish, and baked goods. The man with the keys is the Market Master. It is his responsibility to see that all runs smoothly within the Market.

In 1870 a city ordinance was passed which states, ". . . The Mayor shall appoint a Market Master, whose duty it shall be to attend the market during market hours, and such other times as shall be necessary . . .; he shall prevent the sale of or exposing to sale all unsound and unwholesome provisions . . ." The responsibility of keeping the market clean and the removal of snow were also given to the Market Master.

The Market belongs to and reflects the Lancaster community. The quality that is Central Market is expressed not only in the magnificent building which houses it, but also in the food and wares that are sold there—much of it home-grown and home-prepared from Lancaster's truck farms, home bakeries, and butcher shops. May it continue as it was designated in the City of Lancaster's charter: "to have, hold, and keep . . . market . . . in every week of the year forever!"

Market Days and Hours

Central Market is open from 6:00 a.m. to 4:30 p.m. on Tuesdays and Fridays, and from 6:00 a.m. to 2:00 p.m. on Saturdays. That schedule changes if Christmas or New Year's Day falls on Tuesday, Friday, and Saturday. An extra market day may be added during special holiday weeks. Central Market is located just off the northwest corner of Penn Square in the center of Lancaster City.

APPETIZERS AND BEVERAGES

◆

Belgian Endive and Chevre Appetizer
Makes 8-10 servings

1/3 cup English walnuts, finely chopped
2 Tbsp. butter
8 oz. goatsmilk cheese (chevre), preferably from a 1 kilo log
1-2 Tbsp. walnut oil
1-2 Tbsp. lemon juice
5 heads Belgian endive (to yield 50 well-shaped leaves or spears)
fresh red pepper strips for garnish

1. Sauté English walnuts in butter and brown to your taste. Set aside.
2. Mix goatsmilk cheese with walnut oil and lemon juice. If mixture is of spreading consistency, add 3/4 of the walnuts. If mixture is too firm, add a bit more walnut oil and lemon juice.
3. Spread cheese mixture on endive leaves and arrange in a sunburst pattern on a tray or dish. Sprinkle with remaining walnuts.
4. Use fresh red pepper strips to add color.

—*Sam Neff, S. Clyde Weaver, Inc.*

The North American, Philadelphia, Sunday, July 5, 1908

How Is This for a Housewife's Paradise?

If there is a paradise for the market goer, it should be Lancaster. The fame of the fair city and its wonderful markets has spread beyond the borders of the state. Many Philadelphians go there to purchase supplies for their tables.

Fresh and delicious from the surrounding country, these supplies come every market day, and the prices prevailing are astonishingly cheap, when compared with those of larger cities. Market Day in Lancaster is an institution, and one of which the pretty city is justly proud. And its busy scenes are full of interest for the chance visitor.

Beginning about 1 o'clock every market morning, miscellaneous processions of vehicles from various directions clatter and rumble into Lancaster.

Entering the city, the wagons pass down tree embowered streets, glimmering with the fitful blue luster of electric lamps. Closed shutters frown down upon the picturesque drivers of the wagons—men with patriarchal beards and broad-brimmed hats and women huddled up on the seats wearing plain dresses with peaked capes and plain bonnets.

Fresh Asparagus wrapped with Prosciutto or Westphalian Ham

asparagus
prosciutto or Westphalian ham

1. Blanch asparagus. Immerse it in ice water so it doesn't get too soft.
2. Wrap spears of asparagus with half a slice of prosciutto or Westphalian ham.
—*Sam Neff, S. Clyde Weaver, Inc.*

Asparagus in a Blanket

horseradish cheese spread, softened to room temperature
slices of boiled ham or roast beef
asparagus spears, parboiled

1. Spread horseradish on meat slices.
2. Roll each slice around a spear of asparagus.
3. Serve as an appetizer or party dish.
—*Carol Martin Hottenstein, C.Z. Martin Sons*

Garlic Gilroy

Makes 6-8 servings

1 bulb "elephant" garlic
olive oil
salt to taste
pepper to taste
1 loaf sourdough bread, baguette style, sliced thickly
8 oz. mascarpone cheese

1. Chop off garlic stem. Leave whole and unpeeled.
2. Drizzle garlic bulb with olive oil, salt, and pepper.
3. Place bulb in small baking dish and cover with foil.
4. Bake at 325° for 30-40 minutes, until soft and tender.
5. Grill or toast bread slices.
6. While hot, spread with mascarpone.
7. Squeeze garlic bulb to release cloves.
8. Spread soft cloves over hot bread and cheese.
—*Cindy Cover, Plum Street Gourmet*

Spinach Balls
Makes 10 dozen small balls

20 oz. spinach, chopped, cooked, and drained
8 oz. herb-seasoned croutons
1/2 cup Parmesan or Romano cheese, grated
1-2 large onions, chopped finely
1 tsp. garlic salt
1 tsp. thyme
6 eggs
3/4 cup margarine or butter, melted
pepper to taste

1. Mix all ingredients well.
2. Chill overnight.
2. Shape into small balls, about 1-1½".
3. Bake at 350° for 20 minutes on an ungreased cookie sheet.

—*Melissa Nolt, S. Clyde Weaver, Inc.*

Celery Snack

For your next pot-luck or covered dish meal, consider a tray of bleached celery hearts cut into sticks. Stuff them with vegetable cream cheese or peanut butter, or dunk them in your favorite dip. Dill is an excellent choice and can be mixed with plain low-fat yogurt instead of sour cream. Celery is available year-round, and good Lancaster County homegrown celery is usually available from September through February.

Homegrown celery hearts have been a favorite with folks from Lancaster County for years—especially for Thanksgiving and Christmas dinners. This golden celery is not bitter. It is very tender, not stringy, and has a sweet, almost nutty, flavor.

—*Angie Shenk, Hodecker Celery Farm*

Remedy for Sour Pusses

cucumbers	sugar
cider vinegar	spices
salt	

Hand a jar of Sour Puss Pickles to someone who is sour or a grouch. Our customers tell us it turns the grouch into a smile.

—*Scot Sturtevant, Pennsylvania Pickle Company*

Stuffed Mushrooms

1 lb. large mushrooms
1/3 cup Parmesan cheese, grated
1/2 cup bread crumbs
1/4 cup onion, grated
2 cloves garlic, minced
2 Tbsp. parsley, chopped
salt to taste
pepper to taste
dash of oregano
olive oil

1. Wash and dry mushrooms.
2. Remove stems and chop them.
3. Mix together all remaining ingredients.
4. Stuff mushroom caps with mixture.
5. Rub olive oil over bottom of baking dish. Place caps in dish.
6. Bake at 325° for 25 minutes.

—Mary Ellen Campbell, Baskets of Central Market

Zucchini Appetizers

Makes 10-12 servings

3 cups zucchini, unpared and grated
1 cup flour
1 tsp. baking powder
1/2 cup onion, finely chopped
1/2 cup Parmesan cheese, grated
1 Tbsp. dried parsley
1 Tbsp. mayonnaise
1 Tbsp. Old Bay seasoning
dash of pepper
1/4 cup vegetable oil
4 eggs, slightly beaten

1. Mix all ingredients together. Spread into a greased 9 x 13 pan.
2. Bake at 350° for 25 minutes, or until set.
3. Cut into squares and serve.

—Ethel Stoner, John R. Stoner Produce

◆

Relish Bouquet/Edible Centerpiece

carrots
black olives, slivered
celery sticks
red radishes
1 bunch parsley
1 head lettuce
cauliflower pieces
cherry tomatoes

1. Slice carrots with vegetable peeler.
2. Layer 3-4 carrot slices on a toothpick perpendicular to the toothpick. Place a sliver of black olive in center of top carrot.
3. Slice 6 celery sticks half-way down.
4. Cut off one end of each radish. Then slice half-way down on 4 sides of each radish.
5. Chill carrots, celery and radishes in ice water overnight. They should resemble "flowers" by the next day.
6. Layer parsley on lettuce head with toothpicks. Place lettuce head in a soup bowl.
7. Put all vegetable pieces on toothpicks and arrange over lettuce head as a flower arrangement.
> —*Anna Marie Groff, Anna Marie Groff's Fresh Cut Flowers*

Water Chestnut Bacon Wraps

1 lb. lean bacon
2 8-oz. cans whole water chestnuts
1/2 cup brown sugar
1/2 cup ketchup

1. Cut bacon strips in half and cook lightly.
2. Wrap each water chestnut in bacon. Secure with a toothpick.
3. Place the water chestnuts in a glass baking dish.
4. Mix brown sugar and ketchup together. Pour over wrapped water chestnuts.
5. Bake at 350° for 30 minutes.
> —*Anna Marie Groff, Anna Marie Groff's Fresh Cut Flowers*
> —*Dorothy Nolt, Chet's Flower Garden*

Pennsylvania Dutch Appetizer Logs

Makes 10 servings

5¹/2-oz. jar prepared horseradish
8 oz. cream cheese, at room temperature
³/4 lb. sliced Lebanon bologna

1. Partially drain liquid from horseradish. Mix horseradish thoroughly with cream cheese.
2. Spread mixture onto one side of each bologna slice.
3. Roll up each slice of bologna and cut into 3 sections.
4. Insert a toothpick through each piece.
5. Refrigerate until cream cheese and horseradish stiffen. Serve.

—Michael Long, Long's Horseradish

Swiss 'n Bacon Spread

Makes 1¹/2 cups spread

8 oz. Swiss cheese, cubed
¹/4 cup milk
¹/8 tsp. ground pepper
6 slices bacon, cooked crisp, drained, and crumbled
3 Tbsp. green onions, chopped

1. Combine cheese, milk, and pepper in food processor.
2. Blend until smooth.
3. Stir in bacon and onions.
4. Refrigerate to blend flavors.
5. Allow to stand at room temperature about 30 minutes before servings.
6. Serve with biscuits, crackers, toast, bagels, or English muffins.

—Mabel Haverstick, Viv's Varieties

My sister Miriam and I drove to market as teenagers in the 1930s. My mother, father, Miriam, and I picked berries, peas, and vegetables in season, and we also dressed five or six chickens the morning before we went to market, which opened at 2 p.m.

We always had a few baskets of eggs which we sold and put in paper bags, because there weren't any egg cartons. We bunched rhubarb, onions, etc. with string because nobody had rubber bands.

We parked at Hager's parking lot for 25 cents a day. There was a gas pump there, and, if we bought gas, parking was free.

—Helen A. Thomas, Thomas Produce

◆

Hot Crab Dip

Makes 10 servings

8 oz. cream cheese
2/3 cup mayonnaise
2 tsp. Worcestershire sauce
1 Tbsp. grated onion
3 or 4 drops Tabasco sauce
1 can crabmeat
chips

1. Combine all ingredients except chips. Pour into a baking dish.
2. Bake at 350° for 30 minutes, or until bubbly.
3. Cool a bit before serving with dip chips.

—*Joyce G. Slaymaker, Slaymaker's Poultry*

Spicy Turkey Dip

Makes 25 servings

1 lb. ground turkey
3/4 cup onion, chopped
1 clove garlic, minced
8 oz. tomato sauce
1/4 cup ketchup
1/4 tsp. oregano
1 tsp. sugar
1 tsp. cayenne pepper, or more to taste
1 tsp. cinnamon
2 dashes hot sauce, or more to taste
4 tsp. chili powder
1/3 cup Parmesan cheese, grated
8 oz. cream cheese, softened
corn chips or crackers

1. Cook turkey, onion, and garlic until meat browns.
2. Stir in tomato sauce, ketchup, oregano, and sugar.
3. Cover and simmer 10 minutes.
4. Add seasonings. Add Parmesan and cream cheese and stir over low heat until cream cheese melts.
5. Serve warm with corn chips or crackers.

—*Pamela Rohrer, Sensenig's Gourmet Turkey*

Market Shrimp Dip

Makes 3 cups

16 oz. cream cheese
1 lb. medium shrimp, peeled, cooked, and chopped
2 Tbsp. horseradish
3 Tbsp. chili sauce
1 scallion, chopped
juice of one lemon
1 Tbsp. chives, chopped
parsley for garnish
crackers

1. Soften cream cheese and beat until creamy.
2. Add chopped shrimp and mix well.
3. Add seasonings.
4. Garnish plate with parsley.
5. Serve with crackers.

—*Mary Ellen Campbell, Baskets of Central Market*

Chipped Beef Dip

Makes 2 cups

1/4 cup green onions, chopped
1 garlic clove, minced
1 Tbsp. butter or margarine
8 oz. cream cheese, at room temperature
1/2 cup sour cream
1/4 cup light cream
2 1/2 oz. dried beef, chopped
2 Tbsp. fresh parsley
1 Tbsp. prepared horseradish
1 Tbsp. lemon juice
crackers

1. In a 1-qt. bowl, combine onion, garlic, and butter. Microwave on high for 30-60 seconds until butter is melted.
2. Add cream cheese. Microwave on high for 1-1 1/2 minutes until cream cheese softens.
3. Mix in all remaining ingredients except crackers.
4. Chill at least 2 hours. Serve with crackers.

—*Joyce G. Slaymaker, Slaymaker's Poultry*

Dried Beef in a Bread Shell

8 oz. cream cheese, softened
1/2 cup sour cream
1/2 envelope dry onion soup mix
4-6 oz. dried beef, chopped
3/4 cup green pepper, chopped
1 round loaf pumpernickel bread, unsliced

1. Combine all ingredients except bread. Chill mixture.
2. Cut off top of bread. Pull out bread crumbs, leaving outer shell intact.
3. Place chilled dip in center of bread shell. Serve dip with crackers.

—Kitty Longenecker, Givant's Jewish Baked Goods

Baked Taco Dip

Makes 12 servings

8 oz. sour cream
8 oz. cream cheese
1 1/2 lbs. ground beef, browned
16-oz. can refried beans
1.125-oz. pkg. taco seasoning
8-oz. jar taco sauce
8 oz. cheese of your choice, shredded
1 green pepper, chopped
1 onion, chopped
1 tomato, sliced
taco chips

1. Combine sour cream and cream cheese.
2. In a large casserole dish, layer ground beef, beans, seasoning, taco sauce, sour cream and cream cheese, shredded cheese, pepper, and onion.
3. Bake at 350° for 20 minutes.
4. Layer tomato slices over top of casserole.
5. Bake another 10 minutes.
6. Serve with taco chips.

"Very delicious when reheated, too!"

—Hilda M. Funk, Givant's Jewish Baked Goods

Taco Dip

8 oz. cream cheese, softened
16 oz. sour cream
1.125-oz. pkg. powdered taco seasoning
lettuce, torn in small pieces
tomato, chopped
8 oz. cheese, shredded
tortilla chips

1. Beat cream cheese and sour cream together. Add taco seasoning and mix well.
2. Spread on a plate or dish, 1/2-1" thick.
3. Layer lettuce on top of dip. Layer tomatoes on top of lettuce. Sprinkle cheese on top. Serve with tortilla chips.

—*Melissa Nolt, S. Clyde Weaver, Inc.*

Pizza Dip

Makes 10-12 servings

8 oz. low-fat cream cheese, softened
1/2 cup low-fat sour cream
1 tsp. dried oregano
1/8-1/4 tsp. garlic powder
1/8-1/4 tsp. cayenne pepper
1/2 cup plus 2 Tbsp. pizza sauce
1/2 lb. Sensenig's 98% turkey pepperoni and/or turkey chorizo, diced*
1/4 cup green onion, sliced
1/4 cup green pepper, diced
1/2 cup skim milk mozzarella cheese, shredded
corn chips or crackers

1. In a small bowl, beat together cream cheese, sour cream, and seasonings.
2. Spread evenly in a 9" or 10" quiche dish or pie pan. Spread 1/2 cup pizza sauce on top.
3. Mix pepperoni, chorizo, green onion, green pepper, and 2 Tbsp. pizza sauce. Sprinkle over creamed mixture in quiche dish.
4. Bake at 350° for 10-12 minutes. Remove from oven.
5. Top with shredded mozzarella cheese.
6. Bake 5-10 more minutes until cheese is melted and mixture is heated thoroughly.
7. Serve warm with corn chips or crackers.

—*Pamela T. Rohrer, Sensenig's Gourmet Turkey*

* *If it isn't possible for you to shop at Central Market, substitute with lean pepperoni or chorizo.*

◆

Turkey-Cheese Puffs
Makes 4 servings

3 oz. cream cheese with chives, softened
2 Tbsp. butter or margarine, softened
2 Tbsp. milk
2 cups turkey, cooked and chopped (or roast beef, ham, or chicken)
1/8 tsp. pepper
8 oz. refrigerated crescent dinner rolls

1. Combine cream cheese, butter, and milk until smooth. Stir in turkey and pepper.
2. Unroll dough and separate into 4 rectangles. Press perforations to seal.
3. Spoon 1/2 cup turkey mixture in center of each dough rectangle.
4. Moisten edges of each rectangle with water. Bring the 4 corners to the center to cover the filling, pinching the edges to seal.
5. Place puffs on an ungreased baking sheet.
6. Bake at 350° for 20-25 minutes until puffs are golden.
—*Mary Kay McMichael, Givant's Jewish Baked Goods*

Shrimp Cocktail
Makes 6 servings

12 oz. chili sauce
1-2 Tbsp. horseradish
1 Tbsp. lemon juice
1/2 tsp. Worcestershire sauce
1/4 tsp. salt
dash of pepper
36 medium shrimp, cooked and cleaned

1. Combine all ingredients except shrimp. Chill mixture thoroughly.
2. To serve as individual appetizers, mix shrimp with sauce and serve in lettuce-lined cocktail sherbet dishes.
3. For a party snack, fill a large bowl with crushed ice and place a dish of sauce in the center. Arrange shrimp over ice. Serve with picks for dipping shrimp into sauce.
—*Ann F. Kreider, Viv's Varieties*

Pickle Wheels

8 slices boiled ham
8 oz. cream cheese, softened
8 large pickles, drained (dill or sweet)

1. Spread cream cheese on one side of each ham slice.
2. Place a pickle on top of cheese and roll ham slice around pickle. Press edge to seal.
3. Cover and refrigerate for 1 hour. Use a sharp knife to cut each slice into halves or thirds.

—Anna Marie Groff, Anna Marie Groff's Fresh Cut Flowers

Orange Mint Punch

Makes 4-5 qts.

1 gallon boiling water
2 cups mint tea leaves
1 cup sugar
12 oz. frozen orange juice concentrate
1/2 cup lemon juice

1. Pour boiling water over tea leaves. Let stand for 10 minutes.
2. Strain tea. Add sugar, orange juice concentrate, and lemon juice. Stir well.
3. Chill.
4. Serve over ice. Garnish with orange slices and mint sprigs.

—Hilda Funk, Givant's Jewish Baked Goods

Orange Party Punch

Makes about 5 qts.

3-oz. pkg. orange gelatin
1 cup boiling water
2 cups sugar
2 qts. cold water
46 oz. pineapple juice
1 qt. lemon lime soda
1/2 gallon orange swirl ice cream

1. Blend together orange gelatin, boiling water, and sugar.
2. Add cold water and pineapple juice. Mix well.
3. Just before serving, add lemon lime soda and stir in ice cream.

—Kitty Longenecker, Givant's Jewish Baked Goods

◆

Cranberry Punch

Makes about 1 gallon

1½ qts. cranberry juice
6-oz. can frozen orange juice concentrate
6-oz. can frozen lemonade concentrate
1 qt. ginger ale
1 cup sugar

1. Put all ingredients in a 1-gallon jar.
2. Fill jar with water. Shake until sugar and frozen juices dissolve. Chill.
   —*Ann White, Sunflower Foundataion*

Orange Holiday Fruit Punch

Serves 12 for a 1½ hour cocktail party

1 small pineapple
7 qts. fresh orange pineapple juice
1 orange, cut in wedges
12 oz. frozen lemonade concentrate
2 liters lemon lime soda

1. Select a large mold which will hold a small pineapple. Place pineapple in the form.
2. Fill the form with orange pineapple juice to just below the pineapple stem. Add some orange wedges. Freeze for about 3 days.
3. Place frozen mold in center of punch bowl. Add well chilled juice and concentrate. Just before serving, add lemon lime soda.
   —*Gray Sellers, Lancaster Bagel Company & Lancaster Citrus Company*

Holiday Citrus Punch

Serves 12 for a 1½ hour cocktail party

lemons, cut in slices or wedges
8 qts. cranberry apple juice, chilled
42 oz. lemonade concentrate, defrosted but chilled
3 lemons

1. In a mold of your choice, arrange lemon slices or wedges. Fill mold with cranberry apple juice. Freeze.
2. In a punch bowl, combine remainder of cranberry apple juice and lemonade concentrate. Add frozen juice ring with frozen lemons.
   —*Gray Sellers, Lancaster Bagel Company & Lancaster Citrus Company*

Slush Punch

Makes 6-7 qts.

4 cups sugar
6 cups water
juice of 5 oranges
juice of 2 lemons
46-oz. can pineapple juice
6 oz. frozen lemonade concentrate
2-3 liters ginger ale

1. Boil sugar and water together. Allow liquid to cool.
2. Add fruit juices and concentrate.
3. Pour into ice cube trays or into large, flat containers.
4. Fill a punch bowl 2/3 full with the frozen fruit cubes. Add 2-3 liters of ginger ale. Let punch stand about 10 minutes until it is slushy.
—Mary Kay McMichael, Givant's Jewish Baked Goods

Golden Punch

Makes 5 gallons

18-oz. can frozen lemonade concentrate
18-oz. can frozen orange juice concentrate
48-oz. can grapefruit juice
48-oz. can pineapple juice
4 lbs. (8 cups) sugar
water to make 5 gallons punch
ginger ale or lemon lime soda to taste

1. Mix concentrates and juices together. Add sugar, stirring until it is dissolved.
2. Add water to make 5 gallons punch. (If adding ice, do not add as much water.)
3. Add ginger ale or lemon lime soda when ready to serve.

"I like to make an ice ring with the diluted punch. Pour punch into a ring mold, garnish it with tea leaves and maraschino cherries, and then freeze it. It's quite attractive in the punch bowl when you're ready to serve."
—Joanne Warfel, S. Clyde Weaver, Inc.

Orange and Lemon
Iced Meadow Tea

2 1/2 cups water
2 cups sugar
1 cup meadow tea leaves, firmly packed
    (use only tender tips and leaves)
12 oz. frozen lemonade concentrate
4 oz. frozen orange juice concentrate

1. Boil water and sugar for 5 minutes.
2. Pour water over tea. Cover tightly. Let stand for 1 hour.
3. Strain and squeeze out tea leaves.
4. Add frozen lemonade and orange juice to tea water to make concentrate.
5. When serving, dilute 1 part concentrate with 2 parts water.

—Ann F. Kreider, Viv's Varieties

Russian Tea

Makes 20 servings

2 cups sugar
1 qt. water
2 sticks cinnamon
4 oranges, juice and zest
3 lemons, juice and zest
3 cups pineapple juice
5 regular tea bags
2 cups boiling water
2 qts. water

1. Boil sugar, water, and cinnamon sticks together for 20 minutes. Remove cinnamon sticks.
2. Add three fruit juices and zest.
3. Boil gently for 5 minutes. Strain.
4. Prepare tea by steeping tea bags in 2 cups boiling water. Cool.
5. Combine fruit mixture, tea, and an additional 2 qts. of water.
6. Serve hot or cold.

—Mary Ellen Campbell, Baskets of Central Market

BREADS

◆

Maple-Nut Corn Bread with Country Bacon

Makes 8 servings

6 strips double-smoked bacon
1 cup yellow cornmeal
1/2 cup flour
1 tsp. baking soda
1 tsp. baking powder
1 tsp. salt
1/4 cup maple syrup
1/2 cup buttermilk
1/4 cup vegetable oil
2 eggs
1/2 cup pecans, coarsely chopped
vanilla yogurt or maple syrup for topping (optional)

1. Preheat oven to 400°.
2. Fry bacon over medium heat in a heavy ovenproof skillet or pan. When bacon is crisp, pour fat into a small bowl and set aside. Drain bacon on a paper towel, and then crumble coarsely.
3. Combine cornmeal, flour, baking soda, baking powder, and salt in a mixing bowl.
4. In a separate bowl, beat together maple syrup, buttermilk, and oil with eggs.
5. Combine liquid mixture and dry ingredients. Mix well.
6. Combine pecans with crumbled bacon. Add batter to the pecans and bacon.
7. Pour just enough bacon drippings into the skillet to coat the bottom with a thin film. Heat over high flame until hot, but not quite smoking. Pour the batter into the pan.
8. Bake for 20-25 minutes until lightly browned.
9. Serve hot. Vanilla yogurt or maple syrup makes a good topping.
 —*Gene Shaw, customer of John R. Stoner Produce*

Fifty years ago when I was a little girl, my mother and I would board a bus in Lititz and travel to Lancaster. We went to the Plain Clothing Department of Hager's Department Store to deliver ladies bonnets that Mother had sewn at home. After Mother received her pay and the next week's orders, we crossed the street to Central Market. Mother would buy horseradish to be eaten with fresh sausage and potatoes, one of my dad's favorite meals. Today I still enjoy that wonderful aroma of freshly ground horseradish at Central Market.
 —*J. Lorraine Lapp, Minnich's Farm Bakery*

◆

Spicy Corn Muffins
Makes 1 dozen muffins

1 cup cornmeal
1 cup flour
1/4 cup sugar
3 tsp. baking powder
1 tsp. light salt
1/4 cup butter or margarine, softened
1 egg
3/4 cup skim milk
1/4 cup fat-free sour cream
3 Tbsp. Shenk's Red Hot Pepper Relish*

1. Preheat oven to 425°.
2. Mix together cornmeal, flour, sugar, baking powder, and salt. Cut in the butter or margarine.
3. Beat egg in a separate bowl. Mix together with milk and sour cream, blending well. Add relish.
4. Add wet ingredients to dry ingredients. Mix only to dampen.
5. Spoon batter into greased muffin tins, making them 2/3 full.
6. Bake at 425° for 20 minutes, or until toothpick placed in center comes out clean.

"Adds extra zest to traditional Sunday breakfasts. Also delicious when served with chili.

"This dish tastes wonderful and fills you up. It can be served alone for breakfast or accompanying another dish. It's best when served hot out of the oven. Warms you up on a cold winter morning. Great for Sunday morning breakfast."

—*Janden Richards, Shenk's Cheese Co.*

* *If you are unable to shop at Shenk's Stand on Central Market, substitute 1/2-1 tsp. hot sauce.*

◆

Banana-Pineapple Muffins
Makes 2-3 dozen muffins

2 cups sugar
2 eggs
1 1/8 cups oil
2 cups ripe bananas, mashed
2 1/2 cups flour
2 tsp. baking soda
1 tsp. salt
2 tsp. cinnamon
1 cup coconut
8 oz. crushed pineapple, drained
1 cup walnuts

1. Beat all ingredients together in the order listed.
2. Spoon into greased muffin tins.
3. Bake at 350° for 15 minutes.

—*Mary Ellen Campbell, Baskets of Central Market*

Best Ever Banana Muffins
Makes 1 dozen muffins

3 large, ripe bananas
1/2 cup sugar
1 egg, slightly beaten
1 tsp. baking soda
1 tsp. baking powder
1/2 tsp. salt
1 1/2 cups whole wheat flour
1 tsp. vanilla
1/3 cup applesauce *or* 1/3 cup margarine, melted

1. Mash ripe bananas with fork. Add sugar and egg. Mix well.
2. Mix dry ingredients together.
3. Blend together vanilla, applesauce or margarine, and dry ingredients. Fold lightly into banana mixture until well mixed.
4. Pour batter into lightly greased muffin tins.
5. Bake at 375° for 18-20 minutes. Cool 10 minutes before removing from tins.

—*Yvonne Thomas Martin, Thomas Produce*

Fresh Melopita
Makes 8 small loaves

3 cups fresh apples, peeled and chopped
1 cup raisins
1 cup walnuts, chopped
1½ cups vegetable oil
1 cup white sugar
3 eggs
3 cups flour
1 tsp. baking soda

1. Mix fruit and nuts together.
2. In a separate bowl, combine vegetable oil, sugar, and eggs.
3. Mix together dry ingredients. Combine dry mixture with wet.
4. Add fruit and nuts to batter.
5. Pour batter into 8 greased, small loaf pans.
6. Bake for 30 minutes at 350°. Reduce oven to 325° and bake for 15 more minutes.

—*Areti, Areti's Greek Delights*

Cranberry Muffins
Makes 12 muffins

2 cups flour
1½ tsp. baking powder
1 tsp. baking soda
½ tsp. salt
1 cup sugar
1 egg, beaten
½ cup orange juice
2 Tbsp. butter or margarine, melted
2 Tbsp. hot water
1 cup raw, whole cranberries
1 cup nuts, chopped

1. Combine flour, baking powder, soda, salt, and sugar. Set aside.
2. Mix egg, orange juice, butter, and water.
3. Combine gently with dry ingredients.
4. Fold in cranberries and nuts.
5. Pour batter into greased muffin tins.
6. Bake at 325° for 20 minutes.

—*Joanne Mylin, Robert S. Meck Produce*

◆

Cranberry Orange Oat Bread
Makes 1 loaf

1³/4 cups flour
1 Tbsp. baking powder
1/4 tsp. salt
2 eggs
2/3 cup milk
2/3 cup sugar
1 Tbsp. orange rind, grated
1/3 cup orange juice
1/4 cup oil
1¹/2 cups oat flakes
1 cup cranberries, chopped
1¹/2 cups nuts, chopped

1. Mix flour with baking powder and salt.
2. Beat together eggs, milk, sugar, orange rind, orange juice, and oil.
Combine mixture with dry ingredients just enough to moisten flour.
3. Fold in cereal, cranberries, and nuts.
4. Pour into a well-greased 9x5x3 loaf pan.
5. Bake at 350° for 1 hour, or until tester comes out clean. Cool in pan for
10 minutes. Remove from pan and finish cooling on rack.

Note: For easier slicing, wrap bread and store overnight.
—*Joyce G. Slaymaker, Slaymaker's Poultry*

Ice Box Muffins
Makes 2¹/2 dozen muffins

5 cups bran cereal with raisins
5 cups flour
2 tsp. salt
5 tsp. baking soda
2 cups sugar
4 eggs, beaten
1 cup vegetable oil
1 qt. buttermilk (or 1 qt. sweet milk and 1/4 cup lemon juice)

1. Combine cereal, flour, salt, soda, and sugar.
2. Blend remaining ingredients and mix gently into dry ingredients.
3. Pour batter into greased muffin pans.
4. Bake at 375° for 15 minutes.

Note: Unbaked batter can be kept in refrigerator for 6 weeks.
—*Edith Groff, Groff's Homegrown Produce*

◆

Pumpkin Bread

Makes 2 loaves

4 eggs
1/3 cup dark brown sugar
1/2 cup melted butter or margarine, or vegetable oil
19 oz. Shenk's Pumpkin Butter Spread*
2 tsp. baking soda
1/2 cup plain non-fat yogurt
3 1/2 cups flour

1. Preheat oven to 350°.
2. Beat eggs and sugar together in a large mixing bowl.
3. Beat in butter, margarine or vegetable oil. Add Pumpkin Butter Spread.
4. Dissolve baking soda in yogurt.
5. Add yogurt to pumpkin mixture alternately with flour, blending well after each addition.
6. Pour into 2 greased 9x5x3 loaf pans.
7. Bake at 350° for 1 hour and 15 minutes, or until toothpick placed in center comes out clean.

"This flavorful 'quick bread' has a moist, light texture and can be eaten 'just so.' It's also great for dunking in milk at breakfast. Or, spread slices with your favorite preserves and/or cream cheese as an afternoon or evening snack."

—*Janden Richards, Shenk's Cheese Co.*

* *If you are unable to shop at Shenk's Stand on Central Market, substitute the following for the Pumpkin Butter Spread:*

2 cups cooked and mashed pumpkin
2 cups sugar
1 tsp. cloves
1 tsp. nutmeg
1 tsp. cinnamon
1 1/2 tsp. salt
1/2 cup oil

Mix together thoroughly.

Shoppers leaving the farmers markets with full baskets often found their burdens too great to bear. In years gone by, enterprising boys and a few girls waited with their express wagons (or sometimes sleds in winter) around the market houses to offer their assistance. Few of these youngsters were over 12 years old.

◆

Sweet Potato Rolls

Makes 4-5 dozen rolls

2 pkgs. yeast
1/2 cup warm water
1 Tbsp. sugar
1 cup margarine or butter, softened
7-oz. can yams or sweet potatoes, or one whole sweet potato,
    cooked and mashed
1/2 to 3/4 cup sugar (honey may be substituted)
1 Tbsp. salt
2-3 eggs
1 1/2 cups warm water or scalded milk
4-5 lbs. flour

1. Mix yeast, warm water, and sugar until yeast and sugar dissolve. Set aside.
2. Mix all other ingredients together, except flour.
3. Add flour gradually, to make a moderately stiff dough. Dough is best when a thumb dent in the dough retains an impression.
4. Add yeast mixture. Knead.
5. Let rise in a warm, draft-free place until dough doubles in bulk.
6. Punch down and let rise a second time.
7. Shape into rolls and place on a greased pan.
8. Bake at 350-375° for 10-20 minutes.

"This is a favorite recipe because it is almost impossible to ruin. More sweet potatoes or more sugar, or fewer eggs, may be added for a sweeter roll. Almost any variation is forgiving. Tastes great as hamburger rolls or for cold sandwiches."
    —Carole Manderewicz, *Givant's Jewish Baked Goods*

The North American, Philadelphia, Sunday, July 5, 1908

How Is This for a Housewife's Paradise?

By the time the sun rises, more than 1500 farmers will have arrived, and by 10 o'clock possibly from 10,000 to 12,000 people will have purchased their eatables. Considering the size of the city, it is possibly the biggest market in the United States, and, many claim, the cheapest.

At 2 o'clock Saturday morning the doors of the Central Market House are opened; at 3 the buyers begin to arrive. At the other markets people go still earlier. By 9 or 10 the markets are over.

"The people who don't want to get up in the morning," declared a citizen, "go to the afternoon market." This market, however, is largely attended by the families of working men who get paid Saturday morning.

◆

Sticky Buns

Makes 12-15 servings

1 cup pecans, chopped
2 loaves frozen white bread dough, thawed
1 stick butter, melted
large pkg. vanilla pudding (not instant!)
2 Tbsp. milk
2 tsp. cinnamon
3/4 cup brown sugar

1. Grease a 9x13 pan. Sprinkle nuts on the bottom of the pan.
2. Pull thawed bread into walnut-sized pieces. Fill pan with a single layer of bread.
3. Combine all remaining ingredients. Microwave on High for 3 minutes.
4. Pour microwaved mixture over bread dough.
5. Cover and refrigerate overnight.
6. Bake uncovered for 30 minutes at 350°.
7. Cool slightly. Invert on foil to serve.

—Verna Souders, Kauffman's Fruit Farms

Two Hour Bread

Makes 3 loaves

4 cups white bread flour
2 Tbsp. instant yeast
3 cups hot water
1/2 cup sugar
3/8 cup oil
1 Tbsp. salt
2 eggs
4 cups whole wheat flour, preferably a wheat blend

1. Combine white flour and yeast.
2. In a separate bowl, mix water, sugar, oil, salt, and eggs. Add this to flour mixture. Combine with mixer until smooth.
3. Add whole wheat flour. Beat well. You may need to add a little additional flour if mixture is sticky.
4. Let rise 20 minutes in covered mixing bowl. Grease 3 bread pans.
5. Divide dough into 3 loaves and place in greased pans. Let rise 30-35 minutes.
6. Heat oven to 350°. Bake about 30 minutes. If you make rolls, bake about 18 minutes.

—Kathy Funk, Viv's Varieties

◆

Pluckets
Makes 15-20 servings

1 pkg. dry yeast
1/4 cup lukewarm water
1/3 cup sugar
1/3 cup butter, melted
1/2 tsp. salt
1 cup scalded milk
3 eggs
3 3/4 cups flour
3/4 sugar
3 tsp. cinnamon
1/2 cup chopped nuts, optional
melted butter

1. Dissolve yeast in water.
2. Add 1/3 cup sugar, 1/3 cup melted butter and salt to scalded milk. When mixture is cooled to lukewarm, add yeast mix, eggs, and flour to make a stiff dough.
3. Cover and let rise until double in size.
4. Knead down. Let rise again.
5. Roll into small balls of dough.
6. Combine 3/4 cup sugar, cinnamon, and nuts.
7. Dip balls into melted butter and then into sugar.
8. Drop balls into an angel food cake pan. Let rise about 30 minutes.
9. Bake at 400° for 10 minutes. Turn oven to 350° and bake for 30 minutes.
10. Remove immediately and place on a plate. Pluckets taste best when served warm.

—James Nolt, S. Clyde Weaver, Inc.

Market Rules, 1889

• No person shall keep any horse, cart, carriage, wagon, wheelbarrow, or other vehicle in the avenues around the Market House any longer than may be necessary to unload the same and place their goods on the stalls; and all persons occupying stands out of the Market House, and selling from wagons and other vehicles, shall back their vehicles against the curb stone and remove their horses as soon as possible.

SOUPS

◆

Central Market Soup
Makes 4 servings

1 medium onion
1 medium potato
1 medium apple
1 medium bananas
1 medium celery stalk
2 cups chicken stock
1 cup light cream
1 tsp. curry
salt to taste
pepper to taste
chopped chives, to garnish

1. Peel and chop vegetables and fruit.
2. Combine fruit, vegetables, and chicken stock in a large kettle.
3. Simmer until cooked. Blend to a puree.
4. Add cream, curry, salt, and pepper. Cool and chill. Garnish with chives.
   —Mary Ellen Campbell, Baskets of Central Market

Baked Potato Soup
Makes 4-6 servings

4 large baking potatoes
2/3 cup butter or margarine
2/3 cup flour
6 cups milk
3/4 tsp. salt
1/2 tsp. pepper
4 green onions, chopped and diced
12 slices bacon, cooked and crumbled
1 1/2 cups cheddar cheese, shredded
8 oz. sour cream

1. Bake potatoes at 400°. Cool. Remove pulp and set aside.
2. In a heavy pan, melt butter over low heat. Add flour and stir until
smooth. Cook 1 minute. Add milk. Cook over medium heat until thick and
bubbly.
3. Add potato pulp, salt, pepper, 2 Tbsp. green onion, 1/2 cup bacon, and
1 1/4 cups cheese.
4. Cook until thoroughly heated. Stir in sour cream. Add more milk to
desired thickness.
5. Serve with remaining onion, bacon, and cheese on top.
   —Jim Hollenbach, Slaymaker's Poultry

Wilde Soupe

Makes 10 servings

1/2 oz. wild mushroom pieces
1 cup boiling water
2 Tbsp. olive oil
2 Tbsp. butter
1/2 oz. wild mushroom powder
1 rounded Tbsp. dried minced onion
1/2 tsp. dried thyme
1/2 tsp. celery seed
2 Tbsp. flour
8 cups chicken stock
8 oz. basmati and wild rice, mixed
1 bay leaf
1/2 cup light cream
2 Tbsp. bourbon (optional)
fresh parsley, minced

1. Place dried mushrooms in a small bowl and break up any large pieces.
2. Cover with boiling water. Soak for 10 minutes.
3. In a large soup kettle, heat olive oil and butter over medium high heat. Add seasonings and stir for 1 minute.
4. Sprinkle with flour and stir about 1 minute, until well blended.
5. Add the soaked mushrooms and their liquid. Stir constantly until thickened.
6. Add chicken stock, dry rice, and bay leaf. Bring to a boil. Cover with lid slightly ajar. Lower heat and simmer for 1 1/2 hours.
7. Add light cream and bourbon. Simmer 5 minutes.
8. Garnish with fresh parsley. Serve with leafy green salad and a crusty baguette.

—Barbara Zink, The Herb Shop

Ten years ago a customer came to our stand and purchased some craft items. She asked Mother to keep them while she went to get a cup of tea. When she came back we talked a while and learned she was from Australia. It was Thanksgiving week, and we always have Market four days that week. So she came back on Wednesday, and we invited her to spend Thanksgiving with our family at Mother's house. We had 50 people around one table! She was so delighted.

Her family has been to visit us every year since. This year their son was married, so we were invited to his wedding in Australia. We had a wonderful time. You never know whom you'll meet at Central Market, or where you will end up!

—Viv Hunt, Viv's Varieties

Black Bean Soup

Makes 8 servings

2 cups dry black beans
4-6 cups water
soup bone or ham hock, or 4 cups chicken broth
1 green pepper, chopped
2 small onions, chopped
3 garlic cloves, minced
2 tsp. paprika
1 1/2 tsp. cumin
1/4 tsp. chili powder
2 bay leaves

1. Soak or pre-cook beans for 30 minutes. Pour off water.
2. Add 4-6 cups fresh water to beans. Add soup bone or ham hock (or add chicken broth).
3. Add all remaining ingredients.
4. Simmer for 2 hours.
5. Serve with rice.

—*Sara Jane Wenger, Chet's Flower Garden*

Broccoli Cheddar Soup

Makes 4-6 servings

1/4 cup onion, chopped
1/4 cup butter or margarine
1/4 cup flour
1 tsp. salt
1/4 tsp. pepper
1 cup chicken broth
2 1/2 cups milk
2 cups broccoli, chopped and parboiled (fresh or frozen)
1 cup cheddar cheese, shredded

1. In a saucepan, sauté the onion in butter until onion is tender.
2. Stir in flour, salt, and pepper. Cook and stir until smooth and bubbly.
3. Add broth and milk all at once. Cook and stir until the mixture boils and thickens.
4. Add broccoli. Simmer, stirring constantly, until heated through.
5. Remove from heat. Stir in cheese until melted.

—*Mary H. Harnish, Groff's Homegrown Produce*

Country Corn Chowder
Makes 12-14 servings

1 lb. ham, diced
4 potatoes, diced
1 onion, diced
1 green or red pepper, diced
17^1/2-oz. can cream-style corn
17^1/2-oz. can whole kernel corn
17^1/2-oz. can lima beans
2 cups milk
salt to taste
pepper to taste

1. Put ham and vegetables into a 4-qt. pan. Add water to cover.
2. Bring to a boil. Simmer until tender.
3. Add remaining ingredients. Heat just to boiling.
4. Add salt and pepper. Chowder may be thickened with a bit of flour, if desired.
5. Serve with onion rolls or barbeque rolls.
—*Mike Manderewicz, Givant's Jewish Baked Goods*

Flädelsuppe (Pancake Soup)
Makes 4 servings

1^1/2 level cups flour
2 cups milk
2 eggs
1 tsp. salt
lard
3^1/2 pints soup stock
^{1}/3 cup chives, finely chopped

1. Beat flour, milk, eggs, and salt together well to make a thin batter.
2. Warm frying pan or griddle and rub with lard, and then wipe out with a paper towel.
3. Dip batter onto hot pan or griddle to make pancakes. Cook to a golden brown on both sides. Refrigerate pancakes for 30 minutes to cool.
4. Cut pancakes in thin strips and divide equally into soup bowls.
5. Pour boiling hot soup stock into bowls and garnish with chopped chives.
—*Christine Weiss, German Deli*

◆

Holiday Soup
Makes 8-10 servings

1 lb. assorted beans
2 Tbsp. salt
2 qts. water
2 ham hocks
1 large onion, chopped
2 cups canned tomatoes
1 tsp. chili powder
juice of one lemon
pepper to taste

1. Wash beans and place in a large kettle.
2. Cover with water 2" above bean line. Add salt and soak overnight.
Drain.
3. Add 2 qts. water and ham hocks. Bring to a boil.
4. Add onion, tomatoes, chili powder, lemon juice, and pepper. Simmer 3
hours, or cook in a crockpot for 3 hours on high or 5 hours on low.
5. Remove ham from hocks. Cut into bite-sized pieces and return to soup.
—*Carol Martin Hottenstein, C.Z. Martin Sons*

Winter Vegetable Soup
Makes 8-10 servings

1^1/2 cups dried Great Northern beans
4 Tbsp. butter
1 cup onion, finely chopped
3 leeks, white part only, sliced
2 ribs celery, coarsely chopped
5 carrots, peeled and sliced
1 tsp. thyme
1 bay leaf
3 parsnips, peeled and sliced
1 smoked turkey thigh or ham hock
8 cups chicken stock
1/2 small cabbage, shredded
4 garlic cloves, peeled and chopped
1/2 cup fresh parsley
salt
pepper

1. Soak beans overnight in water.
2. Melt butter in a soup pot. Add onions, leeks, celery, and carrots. Cook over
low heat for 25 minutes, until vegetables are tender and lightly browned.

◆

3. Add thyme, bay leaf, parsnips, meat, drained beans, and stock. Bring to a boil. Simmer partially covered for about 1 hour. Remove meat, cut it in small pieces, and add it to the soup again.
4. Add cabbage, garlic, parsley, salt, and pepper. Cook 10 to 15 more minutes.
—*Gail Johnson, customer at Sensenig's Gourmet Turkey*

New England Clam Chowder
Makes 4 servings

4 slices bacon or salt pork
1/2 cup onion, finely chopped
4 medium potatoes, peeled and diced
1 Tbsp. flour
12 oz. minced clams with liquid
1 cup bottled clam juice
1 cup light cream
salt to taste
pepper to taste
1/2 cup whipping cream (optional)
2 Tbsp. parsley, finely chopped

1. In a large, heavy saucepan or skillet, sauté bacon or pork until brown and crisp. Remove from pan. Drain on paper towels Dice or crumble.
2. In the same skillet, sauté chopped onion and potatoes for a few minutes in the bacon drippings. Sprinkle with flour.
3. Add clam juice from cans and bottled juice. Stir to combine.
4. Bring mixture to a boil. Simmer for about 15 minutes, until potatoes are soft. Stir occasionally.
5. Add light cream and season with salt and pepper. Add minced clams.
6. Heat until chowder simmers. Do not boil. Add whipping cream, if desired. Sprinkle with parsley and diced pork or bacon. Serve immediately.

Variation: This can be prepared in the microwave, but add the clams at the last minute so they do not become tough.
—*Joyce G. Slaymaker, Slaymaker's Poultry*

◆

Gourmet Turkey Bean Soup

Makes 4-6 servings

1 lb. mixed dried beans
1 large Sensenig's 98% Fat Free turkey hock*
2 10½-oz. cans low sodium beef broth
2-lb. can whole tomatoes
1 medium onion, chopped
juice of one lemon
1 tsp. chili powder
fresh ground pepper to taste

1. Soak beans overnight. Drain and rinse.
2. Simmer turkey hock in beef broth for several hours.
3. Remove skin and bone from hock. Cut turkey into bite-sized pieces.
Return meat to the soup pot.
4. Add beans, tomatoes, onion, lemon juice, and seasonings to turkey and
broth.
5. Simmer for several hours on low heat until thickened.
6. Serve warm with a salad and bread.

—Cathy Ketterman, Sensenig's Gourmet Turkey

** If you aren't able to shop at Sensenig's Stand on Central Market, substi-
tute a ham hock.*

Ham and Bean Soup

Makes 8 servings

1 lb. boneless ham
1½ cups potatoes, chopped
1½ cups celery, chopped
1½ cups onion, chopped
1 lb. dried navy beans, soaked
salt to taste
pepper to taste

1. In a large pot, cover ham with water and cook until tender. Cool completely. Skim off fat. Cut meat into small pieces. Set aside with broth.
2. Cook potatoes, celery, and onion in 1 cup water until soft. Add navy
beans and cook until soft. Add more water if necessary to keep vegetables
from sticking to pan.
3. Add ham and broth to other ingredients. Add salt and pepper to taste.
4. Serve hot.

—Ruth B. White, Brenneman Farms

Cheesy Chicken Vegetable Soup

Makes 6-8 servings

2 cups zucchini, sliced
1 cup carrots, sliced
small onion, chopped finely
1 tsp. oregano leaves, crushed
2 Tbsp. margarine
10 1/2-oz. can cheddar cheese soup
10 1/2-oz. can cream of potato soup
1 soup can water
3/4 cup tomato juice
1 1/2 cups chicken or turkey, cooked and cubed
1/2 tsp. hot sauce

1. In a large covered saucepan, cook zucchini, carrots, onion, and oregano in margarine until vegetables are tender.
2. Add remaining ingredients.
3. Heat well, stirring frequently.

—*Edna Martin, C.Z. Martin Sons*

Mom's Homemade Chicken Vegetable Soup

Makes 25 servings

1 qt. lima beans
1 qt. corn, white or yellow
1 qt. carrots, diced
1 qt. peas
1 qt. potatoes, diced
1 cup celery, diced
1/2 onion, diced (optional)
1 qt. chicken, cooked and cut in small pieces
1 Tbsp. dried basil
salt to taste
pepper to taste
6 qts. chicken broth

1. Cook vegetables.
2. Combine vegetables with chicken and seasonings. Add broth. Add water if needed for desired consistency.
3. Serve hot.

Variation: Frozen vegetables may be used.

—*Earl Groff, Groff's Homegrown Produce*

Chicken Noodle Soup

Makes 8-10 servings

2 cups chicken, cooked and diced
13 cups chicken broth
1 cup celery, chopped
1 cup onion, chopped
2 large carrots, grated
1 Tbsp. salt
1 Tbsp. dried parsley
12 oz. broad noodles

1. Add celery, onion, carrots, salt, and parsley to broth. Bring to a boil.
2. Add noodles. Cook about 10-15 minutes, until noodles are tender.
3. Add diced chicken. Serve.

—*Carol Martin Hottenstein, C.Z. Martin Sons*

Oven Beef Stew

Makes 8 servings

1 1/2 lbs. beef, finely cubed
1 onion, finely chopped
2 Tbsp. shortening
1 1/2 tsp. salt
1/4 tsp. pepper
2 Tbsp. flour
1 pint tomato juice
2 cups water
4 large potatoes, diced
4 large carrots, chopped
1 qt. green beans

1. In a large saucepan, brown beef and onion in shortening.
2. Add salt, pepper, and flour. Add tomato juice and water.
3. In a greased 2-3 qt. casserole dish, combine potatoes, carrots, and green beans. Pour beef mixture over vegetables. Cover.
4. Bake at 350° for 2 hours or until vegetables are soft.

—*Mary W. Hess*

Beef Barley Soup
Makes 6-8 servings

1 lb. beef cubes or ground beef
1 Tbsp. olive oil
5 cups water
3/4 cup barley
2 cups carrots, sliced
1/2 cup onions, diced
2 stems celery, chopped
2 medium tomatoes, diced
2 cloves garlic, chopped
2 Tbsp. parsley, chopped
salt to taste
pepper to taste

1. Sauté meat in oil until lightly browned.
2. In a large pot combine all ingredients and simmer for several hours, or until barley and meat are tender. Serve.

Note: This soup freezes very well.

—*Ruth Thomas, Thomas Produce*

Cabbage and Beef Soup
Makes 12 servings

1 lb. lean ground beef
1/2 tsp. garlic salt
1/4 tsp. garlic powder
1/4 tsp. pepper
2 celery stalks, chopped
16 oz. kidney beans, undrained
1/2 medium head cabbage, chopped
28 oz. tomatoes, chopped (reserve liquid)
28-oz. tomato can of water
4 beef bouillon cubes
fresh parsley, chopped, to garnish

1. In a Dutch oven, brown beef.
2. Add all remaining ingredients except parsley. Bring to a boil.
3. Reduce heat. Simmer, covered, for 1 hour. Garnish with parsley.

—*Mary H. Harnish, Groff's Homegrown Produce*

◆

Family Goulash

Makes 4 servings

4 oz. fine noodles
1 lb. ground beef
1 medium onion, chopped
2 cups celery, sliced
1/2 cup ketchup
2 1/2-oz. can mushrooms, sliced
14 1/2-oz. can tomatoes
2 tsp. salt
1/4 tsp. pepper

1. Cook noodles as directed on package.
2. In a large skillet, cook ground beef and onions until meat is brown and onions are tender.
3. Stir in drained noodles, celery, ketchup, mushrooms (with liquid), tomatoes, salt, and pepper.
4. Cover and simmer for 30-45 minutes.

—*Ann F. Kreider, Viv's Varieties*

Italian Sausage and Tortellini Soup

Makes 4 qts.

1 cup Spanish onion, chopped
1 cup green pepper, chopped
1/4 cup light olive oil
8 cups low sodium beef broth
1 lb. canned, whole tomatoes, chopped
1 tsp. garlic, minced
1 tsp. parsley
1 tsp. oregano
1 tsp. basil
1/2 tsp. fresh ground black pepper
1 lb. Sensenig's 98% Fat Free turkey Italian sausage, hot or sweet
12 oz. dried cheese tortellini, cooked
Parmesan cheese, freshly ground

1. Sauté onion and green pepper in olive oil until clear, but not browned.
2. Add broth, tomatoes, and seasonings. Simmer for 25 minutes.
3. Cook sausage and then cut into 1/4-1/2" bite-sized pieces.
4. Add sausage and tortellini to soup. Simmer an additional 30 minutes or until hot.
5. Serve in soup crocks. Sprinkle Parmesan cheese on top of each serving.

—*Cathy Ketterman, Sensenig's Gourmet Turkey*

SALADS
AND
RELISHES

German Cucumber Salad

Makes 4-6 servings

Salad:
2 medium cucumbers, sliced
4 green onions, thinly sliced
3 small tomatoes, chopped
2 Tbsp. fresh parsley, snipped

Dressing:
1/4 cup sour cream
1/4 tsp. prepared mustard
2 Tbsp. fresh dill, minced
1 Tbsp. vinegar
1 Tbsp. milk or cream
1/2 tsp. salt
1/2 tsp. pepper

1. In a bowl, combine cucumbers, onions, tomatoes, and parsley.
2. Combine dressing ingredients. Pour over cucumber mixture and toss gently.
3. Cover and chill at least 1 hour before serving.

"Cucumbers are good for the skin!"

—Viv Hunt, Viv's Varieties

Tomatoes and Basil

Makes 6-8 servings

2 lbs. tomatoes
3/4 cup fresh basil, shredded—not chopped—and loosely packed
3 Tbsp. white rice vinegar
3 Tbsp. extra virgin oil
salt to taste
pepper to taste

1. Rinse tomatoes. Slice evenly.
2. Place tomatoes on a large platter.
3. Sprinkle with remaining ingredients and serve at room temperature. Or, allow tomatoes and seasonings to marinate in refrigerator several hours and serve cold.

—Ethel Stoner, John R. Stoner Produce

Tomato and Asparagus Salad
Makes 4 servings

1/4 cup mayonnaise
3 tsp. Dijon mustard
2 tsp. raspberry or white vinegar
1 lb. asparagus, canned or fresh
lettuce leaves
2 hard-boiled eggs, sliced
2 large tomatoes, sliced
lime slices

1. One day before serving salad, prepare dressing. Combine mayonnaise, mustard, and vinegar. Refrigerate overnight.
2. Remove woody end of asparagus. Cook until tender. Drain.
3. Line a plate with lettuce. Top with asparagus, egg slices, tomato, and lime slices.

—*Mary Ellen Campbell, Baskets of Central Market*

Orange and Tomato Salad
Makes 8 servings

2 tomatoes, cut in wedges
5 cups lettuce, torn
4 oranges, cut in sections
1 cup red onion, sliced
1/4 cup pine nuts

Dressing:
1/2 cup orange juice
4 tsp. red wine vinegar
2 Tbsp. vegetable oil
4 tsp. honey
salt to taste
pepper to taste

1. Mix salad ingredients together.
2. Combine dressing ingredients in a glass jar and shake well.
3. To serve, toss salad and dressing together.

—*Mary Ellen Campbell, Baskets of Central Market*

◆

Sunshine Salad

2 1/2 cups salad greens, torn
1 ripe avocado, peeled, diced, and dipped in lemon juice
2 oranges, peeled and sliced in wedges
1 grapefruit, peeled and sliced in wedges
1/2 red onion, sliced thinly

Dressing:
1/3 cup orange juice
2 tsp. red wine or raspberry vinegar
1 Tbsp. vegetable oil
2 Tbsp. honey
salt to taste
pepper to taste

1. Toss salad ingredients together.
2. Blend together dressing ingredients.
3. To serve, drizzle dressing over salad.
—Mary Ellen Campbell, Baskets of Central Market

Caesar Salad

Makes 6-8 servings

1 garlic clove
2 heads Romaine lettuce
3 Tbsp. rice vinegar
juice of one lemon
dash of Worcestershire sauce
1/2 cup olive oil or vegetable oil
3/4 tsp. salt
1/2 tsp. black pepper, freshly ground
1/4 tsp. dry mustard
2 eggs, beaten
3 Tbsp. freshly grated Parmesan cheese
1 cup croutons

1. Crush garlic in salad bowl with back of wooden spoon. Spread garlic around the bowl with the spoon.
2. Add lettuce to bowl. Add vinegar, lemon juice, and Worcestershire sauce. Toss.
3. Add olive oil. Toss.
4. Add salt, pepper, and mustard. Toss.
5. Gently fold in beaten eggs.
6. Add cheese and croutons. Toss.
—Ethel Stoner, John R. Stoner Produce

◆

Caraway Skillet Slaw

Makes 4 servings

4 slices bacon
1/4 cup vinegar
2 Tbsp. green onion, sliced
1 Tbsp. brown sugar
1 tsp. salt
4 cups cabbage, shredded
1 tsp. caraway seeds
cherry tomatoes, as garnish

1. Cook bacon until crisp. Crumble.
2. Reserve 1/4 cup bacon drippings in skillet. (Pour off the rest.)
3. Add vinegar, onion, brown sugar, and salt. Heat thoroughly.
4. Add cabbage and caraway seeds. Toss lightly and cook briefly until cabbage is crisp-tender.
5. Top with bacon and garnish with cherry tomatoes to serve.

—Frances Kiefer, Kiefer's Meats

Layered Spinach Salad

Makes 10 servings

9 oz. refrigerated cheese tortellini
2 cups red cabbage, shredded
6 cups fresh spinach, torn
2 cups cherry tomatoes, halved
1/2 cup green onions, sliced
8 oz. ranch salad dressing
8 bacon strips, cooked and crumbled (optional)

1. Cook tortellini according to package directions.
2. Drain and rinse tortellini with cold water.
3. In a large glass bowl, layer cabbage, spinach, tortellini, tomatoes, and onions.
4. Pour dressing over top.
5. Sprinkle with bacon, if desired.
6. Cover and refrigerate for at least 1 hour before serving.

—Hilda M. Funk, Givant's Jewish Baked Goods

The Southern Market was built in the elaborate Queen Anne style in 1888 at the southwest corner of Queen and Vine Streets. It survived until 1986, but from the 1950s on it suffered a dwindling trade. The building is now used by the Lancaster Chamber of Commerce.

◆

Marinated Vegetable Salad

Makes 8-10 servings

Salad:
1 bunch broccoli, broken into bite-sized pieces
1 head cauliflower, broken into bite-sized pieces
8 oz. fresh mushrooms, sliced
1 green pepper, chopped
1/2 onion, chopped
8-oz. can water chestnuts (optional)

Dressing:
1/2 cup sugar
1/2 cup oil
1/2 cup vinegar
1 pkg. dry ranch-style dressing

1. Combine salad ingredients.
2. Mix dressing ingredients. Pour over salad.
3. Chill salad for at least 24 hours before serving, stirring lightly a few times.

—*Joanne Mylin, Robert S. Meck Produce*

Mixed Vegetable Salad

Makes 8 servings

1 1/2 cups frozen mixed vegetables
15 oz. kidney beans, washed and drained
1/2 cup celery, chopped
1/2 cup onion, chopped
1/2 cup green pepper, chopped
3/4 cup sugar
1/2 cup white vinegar
1 Tbsp. cornstarch

1. Cook the mixed vegetables as directed, about 10 minutes. Drain. Place in a large bowl and cool. Add kidney beans, celery, onion, and green pepper.
2. In a saucepan over medium heat, bring sugar, vinegar, and cornstarch to a boil. Stir constantly, until thickened.
3. Cool slightly. Pour over vegetables. Toss and refrigerate until ready to serve.

—*Kitty Longenecker, Givant's Jewish Baked Goods*

Variation: Reduce vinegar to 1/3 cup and add 2 Tbsp. prepared mustard to dressing.

—*Mary Keeport Breighner, Rudy Breighner*

Heart of Palm Salad
Makes 4 servings

Salad:
15-oz. can Fingerling carrots
14-oz. can heart of palm
2 medium zucchini, sliced
Bibb lettuce, to garnish
bleu cheese, to garnish

Dressing:
2/3 cup salad oil
1/3 cup white vinegar
1 small garlic clove, minced
1 tsp. sugar
3/4 tsp. salt
3/4 tsp. dry mustard
1/8 tsp. black pepper

1. Combine carrots, heart of palm, and zucchini.
2. Blend dressing ingredients. Pour over vegetables, mixing thoroughly.
3. Drain. Arrange on Bibb lettuce. Sprinkle with crumbled bleu cheese.
—*Carol Simon, Baskets of Central Market*

Baked Potato Salad
Makes 12-15 servings

3-4 lbs. potatoes, boiled and sliced
1 lb. cheese, cubed
1/2 cup onion, chopped
1/2 cup celery, chopped
1 Tbsp. parsley
1 cup mayonnaise
1 1/2 tsp. salt
1/2 tsp. pepper
bacon, cooked and broken, to garnish (optional)
olives, sliced, to garnish (optional)

1. Toss all ingredients together except bacon and olives. Place in an oblong greased baking dish.
2. Top with chopped bacon and olives, if desired.
3. Bake at 350° for one hour. Serve hot or at room temperature.
—*Angie Shenk, Hodecker Celery Farm*

◆

Abundantly Herbed Potato Salad
Makes 12-16 servings

Dressing:
3/4 cup extra virgin olive oil
3 Tbsp. tarragon vinegar
1/4 tsp. salt
fresh ground pepper

4 lbs. red-skinned or Yukon Gold boiling potatoes, ping-pong-ball-
   sized, steamed until just tender and quartered
3/4 cup scallions, thickly sliced
1/3 cup flat-leaf parsley, minced
1/3 cup fresh tarragon, minced
2 Tbsp. fresh dill, minced
2 Tbsp. fresh celery leaves, minced
1 lb. green snap beans, steamed and cut in 1" lengths
4 hard-boiled eggs, coarsely chopped

1. Whisk oil with vinegar, salt, and pepper.
2. Place 1/2 cup of dressing in a large bowl. Add potatoes, scallions, parsley,
tarragon, dill, and celery leaves. Add beans and eggs.
3. Marinate at room temperature for at least 30 minutes.
4. Add remaining dressing and additional salt, if necessary.

—Regine Ibold, Regine's Coffee

Potato Salad
Makes 12 servings

6 cups potatoes, cooked and peeled
6 eggs, hard-boiled
1 1/2 cups mayonnaise
1 1/2 tsp. prepared mustard
1 1/2 tsp. vinegar
2 tsp. salt
1 cup sugar
1/4 cup milk
3/4 cup celery, chopped
2 Tbsp. onion, chopped

1. Shred potatoes and eggs together.
2. Combine remaining ingredients. Fold all ingredients together.

—Elsie King, Shreiner's Flowers

Variation: Add 2 celery stems, diced, to potatoes and eggs.

—Becky Ann Esh, Esh's Deli

◆

Red Beet Eggs

Syrup:
3¹/₂ cups vinegar
4 cups sugar
2 tsp. salt
2 cups red beet juice
3 tsp. red food coloring

hard-boiled eggs, shelled
red beets, cooked

1. Blend vinegar, sugar, and salt together until sugar and salt are dissolved. Add juice and coloring.
2. Place hard-boiled eggs and red beets in syrup.
3. Let stand overnight.
4. Serve eggs and beets chilled, as a salad.

—Joyce G. Slaymaker, Slaymaker's Poultry

Layered Chicken Salad

Makes 8-10 servings

4 to 5 cups lettuce, shredded
1 medium cucumber, thinly sliced
1 cup fresh bean sprouts
8-oz. can sliced water chestnuts, drained
¹/₂ cup green onions, thinly sliced
1 lb. fresh pea pods, halved
4 cups cooked chicken, cubed
2 cups mayonnaise
1 Tbsp. sugar
2 tsp. curry powder
¹/₂ tsp. ginger
cherry tomatoes, to garnish
fresh parsley, to garnish

1. Place lettuce in the bottom of a 4-qt. glass salad bowl. Layer cucumber, bean sprouts, water chestnuts, onions, pea pods, and chicken on top.
2. In a small bowl, combine mayonnaise, sugar, curry, and ginger. Spread over salad.
3. Garnish with cherry tomatoes and parsley, if desired.
4. Cover and chill several hours or overnight.
5. Toss lightly before serving.

—Kathy Funk, Viv's Varieties

◆

Chicken Salad

Makes 10 servings

4 cups cooked chicken, diced
1 cup grapes, halved
1 cup apples, chopped
1 cup pineapple, chopped
1 cup nuts, chopped
1 1/2 cups mayonnaise

1. Combine all ingredients. Mix well.
2. Serve on lettuce or piled on sandwich rolls.
—*Helen A. Thomas, Thomas Produce*

Chicken Aspic

Makes 4-6 servings

1/4 cup cold water
1 env. unflavored gelatin
1 1/2 cups hot chicken stock
1/2 tsp. salt
1 hard-boiled egg, sliced
chives to taste
1 cup chicken, chopped
1 cup vegetables (cooked peas, carrots, etc.)
1/2 cup pimientoes or green pepper, chopped
hard-boiled egg slices
pickle chunks
tomato slices

1. Pour cold water in a bowl. Sprinkle gelatin on top. Add hot stock. Stir until gelatin dissolves. Add salt. Cool.
2. Rinse 4-cup mold in cold water. Pour a thin layer of liquid from Step 1 into mold. Place egg slices and chives in mold. Let this stiffen slightly.
3. When set, add chicken, vegetables, and pimientoes to remaining liquid. Pour into mold. Chill.
4. Unmold on lettuce with tomato and hard-boiled egg slices and pickle chunks around the sides. Serve with mayonnaise, if desired.
—*Roberta B. Peters, Pennsylvania Dutch Gifts*

Turkey Sausage Salad

Makes 6-8 servings

1 lb. new potatoes
3 Tbsp. vinegar
1/2 tsp. salt
fresh ground pepper
2 tsp. Dijon mustard
7 Tbsp. oil
1 small head green cabbage
6 scallions, sliced into rounds
1 1/2 lbs. turkey sausage (Sensenig's 98% Fat Free gourmet turkey*)
tomatoes, to garnish

1. Scrub potatoes and cook them in boiling, salted water until tender. Drain. Return to pan.
2. Shake potoates over warm burner for 2 to 3 minutes to dry out.
3. In a small bowl, mix the vinegar, salt, pepper, and mustard together. Stir in oil, blending well. Separate the dressing into two bowls.
4. Slice warm potatoes and toss gently into half of the dressing. Cover and let stand.
5. Shred cabbage finely and toss with remaining dressing and scallions. Cover and let stand.
6. Place sausage in a skillet and cover with water. Simmer for 10 to 15 minutes, or until cooked. Drain and slice sausage. Refrigerate.
7. Combine cabbage, potatoes, and sausage in a large bowl. Mound in the center of a deep serving dish and surround with thick slices of ripe tomatoes. Serve with biscuits and strawberry pie.

—*Kathleen Peck, customer at Sensenig's*

* *If you are not able to shop at Central Market, substitute lean sausage for Sensenig's 98% Fat Free variety.*

As I was growing up, I tended market with my parents, Rohrer and Mary Groff. Customers always appreciated the freshest vegetables they could buy. Of course, my parents tried their best to grow and harvest their crops as close to the time of selling as possible. They made sure each vegetable was washed with the greatest care and kept fresh in ice to assure a delicate, delectable, and eye-catching item to please the best of customers. Today as I work with my father, we continue to raise organically grown vegetables and sell them as fresh as possible. Our crops are still grown by us on our own farm. The customer must be satisfied! Thanks, Pop and Mom!

—*Earl Groff, Groff's Homegrown Produce*

◆

Smoked Turkey Salad

Makes 6 servings

1 lb. smoked turkey breast
3/4 cup mayonnaise
3 Tbsp. celery, finely diced
2 Tbsp. onion, grated
1 Tbsp. cider vinegar
1 tsp. sugar
1/4 tsp. salt
dash of Worcestershire sauce

1. Coarsely grind turkey breast. Place ground meat in a large mixing bowl.
2. Add remaining ingredients. Mix well.
3. Refrigerate 1 hour before serving in sandwiches, or as a salad on lettuce leaves.

—Jim Hollenbach, Slaymaker's Poultry

Tuna Nicoise

Makes 4-5 servings

1/4 cup red wine vinegar
1/4 cup shallots
1/4 cup fresh parsley, chopped
2 Tbsp. Dijon mustard
1/2 tsp. salt
pepper to taste
1/2 cup olive oil
1 small head lettuce
1/4 lb. fresh green beans, cooked and cooled
8 small red potatoes, cooked and sliced
3 6-oz. cans tuna, drained
1/3 cup Greek olives
2 eggs, cooked and sliced
4 anchovy fillets
tomato slices (optional)

1. Beat together vinegar, shallots, parsley, mustard, salt, and pepper. Gradually beat in oil.
2. Line individual plates with lots of lettuce leaves. Place beans, potatoes, tuna, olives, eggs, and anchovies on top.
3. Decorate with tomato slices for color.
4. Drizzle dressing over each plate.

—Mary Ellen Campbell, Baskets of Central Market

Taco Salad

Makes 6 servings

1 lb. ground beef
1 onion, chopped
15-oz. can red kidney beans
1 tsp. salt
1/2 tsp. pepper
1 head lettuce, torn
2 large tomatoes, chopped
grated cheese
black olives, sliced (optional)

1. In a skillet, brown ground beef and onion. Remove from heat.
2. Stir in kidney beans, salt, and pepper.
3. In a large salad bowl, combine lettuce, tomatoes, cheese, and olives.
4. Blend meat and salad mixtures together.
5. Serve with tortilla chips and chili tomato sauce.

—Ethel Stoner, John R. Stoner Produce

Chili Tomato Sauce for Taco Salad

Makes 3 cups

2 Tbsp. salad oil
1 medium onion, minced
15 oz. tomato sauce
1/2 cup salsa (mild, medium, or hot)
1-2 Tbsp. chili powder
1/4 tsp. oregano
1 tsp. salt
1 Tbsp. garlic powder

1. In a heavy saucepan warm salad oil and sauté onions until just yellow.
2. Add remaining ingredients and blend together.
3. Cover and simmer for a few minutes.
4. Cool and serve over taco salad.

—Ethel Stoner, John R. Stoner Produce

The Western Market occupied the southeast corner of Orange and Pine Streets. It was built in 1882 and contained about 180 stalls. Like the Eastern Market it enjoyed a rather brief existence and closed about 1920. The building still survives, but the second floor was destroyed by fire in 1942 (it was then being used as a roller skating rink).

◆

Veggie-Fruit-and-Nut Mix

Makes 6 servings

6 oz. lemon gelatin
1 cup boiling water
1 cup cold water
1 cup cheese, grated
1 cup celery, diced
1 cup cabbage, shredded
1 cup apples, chopped
1/2 cup nuts, chopped

1. Dissolve lemon gelatin in boiling water. Add cold water. Cool until syrupy.
2. Add all other ingredients. Pour into 9x13 pan or mold. Chill until firm.
3. Serve on lettuce with mayonnaise.

—*Helen A. Thomas, Thomas Produce*

Campbell's Corn Relish

Makes 6 pints

1 qt. raw corn, cut off the cob
3 cups cabbage, grated
1 cup celery, chopped
2 red bell peppers, chopped
2 green peppers, chopped
1 onion, chopped
1 cup sugar
2 Tbsp. dry mustard
3 cups vinegar
2 tsp. salt

1. Blend all ingredients together and cook for 15 minutes.
2. When mixture boils, pack in sterile jars, and seal.

—*Mary Ellen Campbell, Baskets of Central Market*

Gingered Fruit Salad

Makes 8 servings

2 oranges, peeled and sectioned
2 tart apples, peeled, cored, and chopped
2 peaches, sliced
1 cup strawberries, halved
1 cup plain nonfat or lowfat yogurt
2 Tbsp. brown sugar, packed
1/2 tsp. ginger

1. In a large bowl, toss fruit together.
2. In a small bowl, combine yogurt, brown sugar, and ginger. Blend well with a fork. Fold two mixtures together.

—*Ethel Stoner, John R. Stoner Produce*

Strawberry Fruit Salad

Makes 4-6 servings

6 oz. cherry or strawberry gelatin
1 1/4 cups boiling water
1 pint frozen strawberries
1 cup frozen blueberries or 3 bananas, crushed
20-oz. can crushed pineapple, drained

1. Add boiling water to gelatin. Stir until dissolved.
2. Add strawberries and blueberries, or bananas. Stir to thaw frozen fruit.
3. Add crushed pineapple. Mix well. Pour into serving dish or mold. Chill.

—*Melissa Nolt, S. Clyde Weaver, Inc.*

My grandpa Isaac Keeport and my uncle Daniel B. Keeport used to sell on the curb market. When the market house was built, Grandpa bought the stand where we stand now. My parents raised produce, made cup cheese, butter ball cheese, and schmierkase. They also sold eggs in paper bags, instead of the boxes used now. In the summer we sold chickens off a tray of ice at the stand. Chickens were sold by the weight of your hand.

When I was a little girl, Daddy got up very early in the morning on market days and packed the truck. I asked to go along. He said I could if I was ready on time. Sometimes I was ready on time; other times I didn't make it. I used to like the ice cream stand and the candy stand. Those were the good days.

—*Rudy and Mary Breighner, Rudy Breighner*

◆

Mom's Refrigerator Pickles

3 qts. cucumbers, thinly sliced
2 large onions, sliced
2 green peppers, thinly sliced
1 tsp. celery salt
2 cups white vinegar
3 cups sugar
1/3 cup salt

1. Mix ingredients together. Let stand in a covered plastic container.
2. Pickles are ready in one day and will last a year in the refrigerator.
3. You may add cucumber slices to the syrup at any time.

—Mary Keeport Breighner, Rudy Breighner

Seven-Day Sweet Pickles

7 lbs. medium-sized pickles
water to cover
1 qt. vinegar
8 cups sugar
2 Tbsp. salt
2 Tbsp. mixed pickle spices
2 drops green food coloring

1. Wash pickles and cover with boiling water. Let stand 24 hours and drain.
2. Do this for 4 days, using fresh water each time.
3. On Day 5, cut pickles in 1/4" chunks.
4. Combine vinegar, sugar, salt, spices, and food coloring.
5. Bring liquid to a boil and pour over sliced pickles. Let stand 24 hours.
6. On Day 6, drain syrup and bring to a boil. Pour over pickles.
7. On Day 7, drain off syrup and bring to a boil.
8. Add pickles and bring to a boiling point.
9. Pack into hot sterilized jars and seal.

"I found the secret is to move these into the refrigerator after they have cooled each day. They stay crisp and are much better. If you are busy and can't change the water every day, they are fine in the refrigerator."

—Miriam Harnish, Groff's Homegrown Produce

◆

Garlic Pickles

Makes 4 quarts

pickles, enough to fill 4 qt. jars
8 garlic cloves
4 heads dill
2 cups vinegar
2 cups water
3 cups sugar
2 tsp. salt

1. Slice pickles and fill each jar to the neck.
2. Place 2 garlic cloves and 1 head of dill in each jar.
3. Heat vinegar, water, sugar, and salt, and fill each jar with this liquid.
4. Place jars in a hot water bath and boil for 5 to 10 minutes.

—Elsie S. King, Shreiner's Flowers

14-Day Sweet Pickles

1$^{1/2}$ cups salt
50 medium-sized pickles
$^{1/4}$ cup alum
1 cup horseradish
24 cups sugar
2 qts. white vinegar
1$^{1/2}$ tsp. whole cloves
1$^{1/2}$ tsp. celery seed
1$^{1/2}$ sticks cinnamon

1. Dissolve salt in warm water deep enough to cover the pickles. Soak pickles in this solution for 7 days.
2. On Day 8, drain pickles; then cover them with boiling water.
3. On Day 9, drain pickles, and cut them into slices. Add alum and horseradish to the pickles; then cover them with boiling water.
4. On Day 10, drain and cover them again with boiling water.
5. On Day 11, make syrup by combining sugar, vinegar, and spices and bringing mixture to a boil. Drain pickles of water and cover with syrup.
6. On Day 12, drain syrup, bring it to a boil, and pour over pickles.
7. On Day 13, reheat syrup and pour over pickles again.
8. On Day 14, pack pickles into sterilized jars. Pour boiling syrup over pickles and seal.

"These are crisp and delicious pickles. Every year Grandpa Leaman would ask me to can some especially for him because they were his favorite!"
—Arlene Leaman, S. Clyde Weaver, Inc.

VEGETABLES

◆

Asparagus with Pimientoes
Makes 4-6 servings

1 lb. fresh asparagus, trimmed
1/4 cup dried bread crumbs
3 Tbsp. butter
2 Tbsp. Parmesan cheese, grated
1 Tbsp. pimientoes, chopped

1. In a saucepan over medium heat, cook asparagus in boiling salt water until tender.
2. In a skillet, brown bread crumbs in butter.
3. Drain asparagus. Place in a serving dish.
4. Sprinkle with bread crumbs, cheese, and pimientoes.
—Mary S. King, Shreiner's Flowers

Baked Lima Beans
Makes 10-12 servings

1 lb. lima beans (dry)
1/2 lb. bacon
1/2 cup onion, minced
3/4 cup celery, chopped
3/4 cup sweet molasses
1/2 cup brown sugar
1/2 cup ketchup
1 1/2 tsp. dry mustard
1 1/2 tsp. salt
1 1/2 cups cooking liquor or tomato juice
1 1/2 Tbsp. Worcestershire sauce
1/8 tsp. pepper

1. Wash beans several times. Soak overnight, making sure they are well covered with water.
2. Parboil beans in the water in which they were soaked, adding additional water if necessary. Do not allow beans to become too soft.
3. Fry bacon until crisp. Drain on paper towels. Break bacon into small pieces.
4. Cook onions and celery in bacon drippings until onions become transparent.
5. Mix together all ingredients, saving some bacon for a garnish on top.
6. Bake at 350° for 1 1/2 hours or more, until beans are tender.
—Katie Stoltzfus, Eisenberger's Bakery

◆

Green Beans with Bacon

Makes 4-6 servings

1 qt. green beans
3 slices bacon
1 tsp. salt
water for steaming beans

1. Wash and snap beans.
2. Dice bacon. Fry in heavy saucepan.
3. Add beans, salt, and water to bacon. Cook until beans are tender.

—Ruth B. White, Brenneman Farms

Sweet and Sour Green Beans

Makes 4 servings

6 slices bacon
1/4 cup bacon drippings
6 Tbsp. sugar
1 tsp. prepared mustard
1 Tbsp. vinegar
2 cups cooked green beans

1. Brown bacon and save 1/4 cup of the drippings. Crumble bacon.
2. Add sugar, mustard, and vinegar to drippings. Stir well.
3. Pour sauce and bacon over the green beans and toss.

—Melissa Nolt, S. Clyde Weaver, Inc.

Broccoli Casserole

Makes 4-6 servings

2 bunches of broccoli
1/4-1/2 lb. cheese of your choice, grated
1/4 lb. butter
about 36 snack crackers

1. Cook broccoli until just tender.
2. Melt cheese with butter.
3. Crush crackers.
4. In a greased 2-qt. casserole dish, alternate layers of broccoli, cheese sauce, and crackers.
5. Bake uncovered at 325° for 15-20 minutes.

—Ruth H. White, Sunflower Foundation

Red Cabbage and Apples

6 lbs. red cabbage, shredded
2 lbs. onions, sliced
6 tart Granny Smith apples, sliced and peeled
3 Tbsp. butter
1 cup red wine vinegar
salt to taste
pepper to taste
1-2 tsp. sugar (optional)

1. Sauté cabbage, onions, and apples in butter.
2. When cabbage is wilted, add vinegar and simmer until most liquid is evaporated. Add salt, pepper, and sugar.
3. Serve hot or cold. May be served with grilled meats and/or bratwurst, bockwurst, or German wieners.

—Sam Neff, S. Clyde Weaver, Inc.

Baked Carrots

Makes 6-8 servings

3$^1/_2$ cups carrots, sliced
3 Tbsp. butter or margarine, melted
3 Tbsp. flour
1$^1/_2$ cups milk
$^3/_4$ lb. cheese, sliced or grated

1. Preheat oven to 350°.
2. Cook carrots in a small amount of salted water until tender. Drain and place in a greased 1$^1/_2$-qt. casserole dish.
3. Melt butter in a heavy saucepan. Add flour. Stir until well blended.
4. Slowly add milk, stirring constantly, until a smooth sauce forms.
5. Add cheese and stir until melted.
6. Pour sauce over carrots.
7. Bake until light brown, about 30-35 minutes.

—Ann White, Sunflower Foundation

When I was a small child, my mother took me along to her market stand. One day she went to Watt & Shand, our former department store, to buy yarn and needles. She came back to market and proceeded to teach me how to knit. I guess she thought that would keep me busy, plus keep me out of trouble.

—Frances Kiefer, Kiefer's Meats

◆

Cheese Cauliflower Scallop

Makes 6-8 servings

1 medium head cauliflower, separated into sections and
    cooked until just tender
2 cups medium white sauce (see below)
1 cup sharp cheese, grated

1. Arrange cauliflower in a greased 8x8 baking dish.
2. Pour white sauce over top. Sprinkle with cheese.
3. Bake uncovered for 30-40 minutes at 350°.

Medium White Sauce

2 Tbsp. butter
2 Tbsp. flour
1/2 tsp. salt
1/4 tsp. pepper
1 cup milk

1. Melt butter. Blend in flour and seasonings.
2. Over low heat, gradually pour in milk, stirring until smooth.
3. Continue cooking until sauce thickens, stirring continually.

—Elva E. Martin, Rudy Breighner

Stewed Celery

Makes 3-4 servings

10 stems stewing celery

Sauce:
1 Tbsp. butter
1 Tbsp. flour
1 Tbsp. sugar
1 Tbsp. vinegar
1 egg, beaten
1/2 cup water

1. Cut celery into 1/2" pieces. Cook. Set aside.
2. Melt butter. Stir in flour, sugar, and vinegar.
3. Add 1/2 cup water to beaten egg. Combine with butter mixture.
4. Cook a few minutes to thicken. Add celery.

"This tastes especially good on toast."

—Edith Groff, Groff's Homegrown Produce

Corn Pudding

Makes 6 servings

2 cups corn, grated (fresh or frozen)
2 Tbsp. sugar
1 tsp. salt
2 Tbsp. flour
2 Tbsp. butter, melted
2 eggs, beaten
1 cup milk

1. Prepare corn and add sugar, salt, flour, and melted butter.
2. Stir in beaten eggs and milk.
3. Pour mixture into a greased 1¹/2-2 qt. baking dish.
4. Bake at 350° for 40 minutes or until center is set.

—*J. Lorraine Lapp, Minnich's Farm Bakery*

Easy-Baked Eggplant

Makes 4 servings

1 medium eggplant
butter
cracker crumbs
salt to taste

1. Peel and slice eggplant very thinly.
2. Spread each side of each slice with butter. Sprinkle cracker crumbs on each side of the eggplant slices.
3. Place slices in a long baking dish or cookie sheet, so that slices do not overlap. Sprinkle with salt.
4. Bake at 375° for 10-15 minutes.

—*Earl Groff, Groff's Homegrown Produce*

Remedy for Removing a Splinter

1 slice of bacon

Lay bacon on the splinter for about 5 minutes. The fat will help to remove it!

—*Frances Kiefer, Kiefer's Meats*

◆

Eggplant Casserole

Makes 4 servings

2 eggs
2 cups milk
3 cups bread cubes
1½ cups eggplant, cooked and mashed
⅔ cup sharp cheese, grated
3 Tbsp. butter, melted
1 tsp. salt
pinch of pepper
1 cup buttered bread crumbs

1. Blend eggs and milk.
2. Moisten bread cubes with the milk and egg mixture.
3. Add all remaining ingredients, with the exception of the buttered bread crumbs.
4. Place in a 2-qt. buttered casserole dish.
5. Top casserole with buttered bread crumbs.
6. Bake at 350° for 1 hour.

—*Mrs. Martha Flory, C.Z. Martin Sons*

Mushrooms and Bacon

Makes 4 servings

3-4 slices bacon, diced
1 lb. fresh mushrooms, sliced
pepper to taste

1. In a skillet, sauté bacon over medium-high heat 5-7 minutes, until almost crisp. Drain all but ½ tsp. drippings.
2. Add mushrooms and sauté.
3. Cool 4-5 minutes. Season with pepper.
4. Fold crumbled bacon into mushrooms; then serve on toast as breakfast or luncheon dish.

—*Joyce G. Slaymaker, Slaymaker's Poultry*

◆

Stuffed Mushrooms
Makes 6 servings

12 large mushrooms
3 slices bacon
1 large onion, chopped fine
1/4 cup green pepper, chopped fine (optional)
1 cup stale, soft bread crumbs
2 Tbsp. parsley, chopped
1/2 tsp. seasoned salt
chicken stock to moisten
salt to taste
pepper to taste

1. Remove mushroom stems and chop very finely.
2. Cook bacon. Drain it, leaving 2 Tbsp. dripping in the pan. Set bacon aside.
3. Add chopped mushroom stems, onion, and green pepper to bacon drippings. Sauté until tender.
4. Add bread crumbs, crumbled bacon, parsley, salt, and chicken stock to pan.
5. Season with salt and pepper.
6. Stuff mushroom caps with this mixture. Place them in a shallow pan with about 1/4" of chicken stock.
7. Bake at 325° for 25-30 minutes.

—Jim Hollenbach, S. Clyde Weaver, Inc.

Oven Roasted Potatoes a la Provence
Makes 6-8 servings

2 lb. potatoes, unpeeled and cut in large chunks
about 4 Tbsp. extra virgin olive oil
1 1/2 tsp. Herbes de Provence
salt to taste
pepper to taste

1. Preheat oven to 400°.
2. Toss potatoes in enough olive oil to lightly coat them.
3. Sprinkle potatoes with Herbes de Provence. Toss again.
4. Place potatoes in a large roasting pan.
5. Roast potatoes for about 40 minutes, stirring occasionally. Season with salt and pepper.

—Bonnie Sullivan, The Herb Shop

◆

Parmesan Baked Potatoes

Makes 8 servings

6 Tbsp. butter, melted
3 Tbsp. Parmesan cheese, grated
8 medium red potatoes, unpeeled and halved lengthwise

1. Pour butter into a 9x13 baking pan.
2. Sprinkle cheese over butter.
3. Place potatoes cut-side down on top of cheese.
4. Bake uncovered at 400° for 40-45 minutes, or until tender.

—Edith Groff, Groff's Homegrown Produce

Refrigerator Mashed Potatoes

Makes 12 servings

5 lbs. potatoes, peeled
2 3-oz. pkgs. cream cheese
1 cup sour cream
2 tsp. onion salt
1 scant tsp. salt
1/4 tsp. pepper
2 Tbsp. butter

1. Cook potatoes in boiling salt water. When potatoes are soft, drain them and mash them until smooth.
2. Add remaining ingredients. Beat until light and fluffy. Cool.
3. Cover mixture and place in refrigerator. Potatoes may be used anytime within 2 weeks.
4. To prepare, place potatoes in a 2-qt. greased casserole dish. Dot with butter.
5. Bake at 350° until thoroughly heated, approximately 30-45 minutes.

Note: This is especially good with Irish Cobbler Potatoes!

—Miriam Harnish, Groff's Homegrown Produce

Variation:
1. Add 2 tsp onion, finely chopped, to mashed potatoes.
2. If potatoes seem stiff, add 1/4-1/2 cup hot milk and blend in.

—Elva E. Martin, Rudy Breighner

Scalloped Cheese Potatoes

Makes 6 servings

1/2 cup butter
1/2 cup onion, chopped
1 tsp. mustard
1 tsp. salt
1/4 tsp. pepper
1/4 cup milk
1/4 cup Velveeta cheese
6 medium potatoes, cooked and sliced
1/4 cup buttered bread crumbs

1. Melt butter in a saucepan. Add onion, mustard, salt, pepper, milk, and cheese. Place potatoes in a casserole dish. Pour cheese sauce over potatoes.
3. Sprinkle bread crumbs on top.
4. Bake at 350° for 45 minutes.

—Lorraine Good, Eisenberger's Bakery

Baked Potato Casserole

Makes 8 servings

1/4 lb. butter
2 10 1/2-oz. cans cream of chicken soup
1 1/2 cups milk
8 medium potatoes
1 medium onion
1 cup cheddar cheese, grated

1. Melt butter. Stir in soup and milk until smooth.
2. Cut potatoes and onion into thin slices.
3. Place a layer of potatoes and onion in a greased baking dish. Top with half of the soup and milk mixture.
4. Repeat Step 3, using all the remaining potatoes, onion, soup, and milk.
5. Top with cheddar cheese.
6. Bake at 350° for 2 hours.

—Helen A. Thomas, Thomas Produce

◆

Potato-Turnip Scallop

1½ cups potatoes, scrubbed and sliced thin
1½ cups turnips or rutabagas, scrubbed and sliced thin
1 medium onion, sliced into thin rings
sea salt or table salt
½ tsp. savory
2 Tbsp. minced parsley
2 cups cheese, grated
1 cup bread crumbs
1 cup skim milk

1. Grease a casserole dish. Place half the potatoes on the bottom of the dish. Layer half of the turnips on top, followed by half the onions.
2. Sprinkle with salt. Sprinkle with ¼ tsp. savory and 1 Tbsp. parsley. Cover with 1 cup cheese.
3. Repeat these layers in the same order.
4. Top casserole with bread crumbs. Pour milk over all.
5. Bake uncovered at 350° for 45 minutes or until vegetables are tender.
6. Serve with broccoli or green beans and a salad.

"Turnips have potassium. They're bodybuilders. Turnip juice is good for asthma, sore throat, and bronchial disorders. Daddy loved his garden and was proud to have the first potatoes, peas, and turnips on Central Market."

—*Viv Hunt, Viv's Varieties*

Roasted Root Vegetables

Makes 6 servings

5-6 medium potatoes, cut in quarters
1 turnip, peeled and sliced
2-3 parsnips, peeled and cut in strips
1-2 carrots, cut in crosswise slices
4 Tbsp. olive oil
1 pkg. dry onion soup mix
salt to taste
pepper to taste
garlic powder to taste

1. Preheat oven to 400°.
2. Place vegetables in a plastic bag. Add oil and soup mix. Shake until well coated. Spread vegetables on a greased cookie sheet.
3. Roast in oven for about 20 minutes, or until vegetables are crispy and tender. Turn occasionally.

—*Ethel Stoner, John R. Stoner Produce*

◆

Friday Night Baked Vegetables

Makes 3-4 servings

1½ lbs. red and green peppers, mixed
1 lb. new potatoes, unpeeled
1 large sweet onion
1 head garlic, flattened into cloves, unpeeled
¼ cup olive oil
coarse salt
freshly ground pepper
bunches of fresh thyme or rosemary

1. Cut peppers lengthwise into quarters. Remove seeds and membrane.
2. If potatoes are small, do not cut them. If larger, halve or quarter them.
3. Cut onion into eighths.
4. Place vegetables and garlic in a large, shallow roasting pan. Toss well with olive oil, salt, pepper, and herbs.
5. Bake at 425° for 35 minutes, tossing and shaking every 10 minutes.
6. Serve with French bread. Squeeze garlic out of skin onto each slice.

Variations:
1. Add halved plum tomatoes.
2. Add grated mozzarella at the end of baking, and allow cheese to melt.
3. Add blanched, sauteed sausage pieces.
4. Add partially cooked chicken pieces.

—Regine Ibold, Regine's Coffee

Sweet Potato Patties

Makes 4 servings

1 pint sweet potatoes, mashed
1 egg
1 tsp. salt
2 Tbsp. brown sugar
1 Tbsp. butter
cracker crumbs

1. Cook sweet potatoes and mash them.
2. Add egg, salt, brown sugar, and butter to sweet potatoes.
3. Shape mixture into patties. Roll patties in cracker crumbs.
4. Place patties on a greased cookie sheet.
5. Bake at 350° for 15-20 minutes.

—Edith Groff, Groff's Homegrown Produce

◆

Sweet Potato and Apple Puree

Makes 6-8 servings

2 lbs. sweet potatoes, peeled and cut in 1" pieces
2 Tbsp. unsalted butter
1 cup onion, finely chopped
2 large apples (Granny Smith, Golden Delicious, or Jonagold),
    peeled, cored, and sliced thinly
salt to taste
pepper to taste
3 Tbsp. sour cream, or to taste
freshly grated nutmeg to taste

1. In a large saucepan, cover sweet potatoes with water and then boil them
for about 10-12 minutes, or until tender.
2. Meanwhile, melt butter over medium heat. Cook onion, apples, salt,
and pepper for 5-10 minutes, or until apples are tender, stirring frequently.
3. Drain sweet potatoes. Puree sweet potatoes with the apple mixture until
mixture is smooth. (It may need to be done in 2 batches.)
4. With blender/processor still running, add sour cream, nutmeg, and additional salt and pepper.
5. If a thinner puree is desired, add a bit of hot water while the
blender/processor is still running.
6. Serve hot.

—Gene Shaw, customer of John R. Stoner Produce

Sweet Potatoes with Pineapple

Makes 6 servings

6 medium sweet potatoes, peeled and diced
1/2 cup brown sugar
1/2 tsp. salt
1 Tbsp. cornstarch
1 cup crushed pineapple, undrained
1/2 cup orange soda or orange juice
1/4 cup margarine

1. Cook sweet potatoes until tender. Arrange in a 2-qt. baking dish.
2. In a saucepan, combine the remaining ingredients. Cook to boiling.
3. Pour mixture over potatoes.
4. Bake at 350° for 20-25 minutes.

—Sara Jane Wenger, Chet's Flower Garden

◆

Sweet Potato Casserole

Makes 6-8 servings

Casserole:
4-5 sweet potatoes, peeled, cooked, and mashed
1/2 cup sugar
4 Tbsp. butter or margarine, melted
1 1/2 tsp. vanilla
2 eggs

Topping:
3/4 cup packed brown sugar
1/3 cup flour
4 Tbsp. butter, melted
1 cup pecans, chopped

1. Mix all casserole ingredients together. Place in a greased 2-qt. casserole dish.
2. Mix topping ingredients together with a fork. Sprinkle topping over sweet potatoes.
4. Bake at 350° for 45 minutes.

—*James Nolt, S. Clyde Weaver, Inc.*

Squash with
Browned Butter and Mace

Makes 4 serving

2 pints squash (any variety), peeled and cubed in 3/4" pieces
4 Tbsp. butter
1/4 tsp. mace, or more to taste
Parmesan cheese, grated, to garnish

1. Steam squash until firm to tender. Salt to taste. (Do not overcook squash or it will become mushy.)
2. Brown butter, in a separate pan. Add mace. Pour over steamed squash.
3. Serve with grated Parmesan cheese.

"We enjoy this at Thanksgiving because it adds color and aroma. Mace comes from the outer coating of nutmeg. It is a bit spicy and has a fantastic aroma. It is not as sweet as nutmeg."

—*Sam Neff, S. Clyde Weaver, Inc.*

◆

Grilled Radicchio and Assorted Greens

1 head radicchio
1 bunch arugula, and/or 2 spears Belgian endive,
    and/or 1 bunch watercress
olive oil
balsamic vinegar
8-10 slices prosciutto or pancetta

1. Clean radicchio and make pairs of cupped leaves, one leaf forming the bottom; the other forming the top.
2. Fill bottom radicchio leaf of each pair with other greens. Close each leaf pocket with its paired piece of radicchio.
3. Drizzle 1/2 tsp. olive oil and 1/4 tsp. balsamic vinegar over each filled leaf. Close each leaf pocket with its paired piece of radicchio.
4. Wrap each radicchio pocket with 1 slice of prosciutto and secure with a long toothpick or skewer.
5. Grill over hot coals or gas grill. (Don't panic when a few flames appear; that is normal!) Radicchio is finished when prosciutto looks crisp like bacon and the leaf ends are a bit charred.
6. Drizzle each pocket with a bit of olive oil and vinegar. Serve warm.

This recipe takes a bit of practice until one learns the balance between the oil marinade on the interior of the leaves and the ideal heat for the grill. It is well worth the effort. I have also baked them in the oven at 500° for 10 minutes.
                                        —*Sam Neff, S. Clyde Weaver, Inc.*

The curb market, developed in the 1820s to relieve the inadequate space in Central Market, was not a random arrangement. City ordinances specified which areas of which streets could be used for marketing. The places were neither occupied by market wagons on a first-come, first-served basis, nor were they free for the taking.

In 1818 the curb market occupied West King Street as far as Prince Street and the whole of Center Square. By 1845 it extended a block in each direction from the Center Square on King and Queen Streets. In 1898 the curb market changed its dimensions again. There were 57 spaces on East King Street, 35 on Duke Street and nine in Center Square. These spaces were auctioned off, the same as those in the market house.

During its final period the curb market extended from Center Square on East King Street to Duke, down Duke to Vine, and west on Vine to Prince where it reached almost to Orange Street. In the same areas, stores and businesses also rented space along the fronts of their buildings to the operators of smaller businesses and their "basket stands."

◆

Baked Rice

Makes 4 servings

2½ Tbsp. butter
2 Tbsp. onion, minced
½ tsp. garlic, minced
1 cup rice, uncooked
2 cups chicken broth
3 sprigs parsley
1 sprig fresh thyme or ½ tsp. dried thyme
½ bay leaf
salt to taste
pepper, freshly ground, to taste

1. Preheat oven to 400°.
2. Melt half of butter in a heavy saucepan. Cook onion and garlic until onion is translucent.
3. Add rice and stir briefly over low heat until grains are coated with butter.
4. Stir in chicken broth, making sure there are no lumps in the rice.
5. Add all seasonings.
6. Cover with a tight lid and place in the oven. Bake exactly 37 minutes.
7. Remove from oven. Discard parsley and thyme sprigs and bay leaf. Using a 2-pronged fork, stir in remaining butter and serve.
—*Joyce G. Slaymaker, Slaymaker's Poultry*

Spinach and Yogurt

Makes 6 serving

1 lb. fresh spinach (or 2 boxes frozen)
1 medium onion, diced
1-2 garlic cloves, crushed
olive oil
½ tsp. turmeric
½-¾ tsp. cumin seeds, ground
¼ tsp. chili powder, mild or spicy
salt to taste
2 cups plain yogurt

1. Steam spinach. Drain.
2. Sauté onion and crushed garlic in olive oil. Add spices. Brown slightly.
3. Add spinach. When spinach is hot, turn off heat. Add yogurt.
4. Slowly reheat if desired, but cooked yogurt will separate!

"We enjoy serving this with roast leg of lamb, with a bit of lemon juice for the lamb and spinach. The dish can also be served cold or at room temperature."
—*Sam Neff, S. Clyde Weaver, Inc.*

◆

Tomato Fritters
Makes 6 serving

3 cups canned tomatoes
1 small onion, minced
1 tsp. salt
1 Tbsp. sugar
4 Tbsp. cornstarch
2 eggs
crushed cracker crumbs
butter or margarine

1. Cook tomatoes, onion, salt, and sugar together for 15 minutes.
2. In a small bowl, mix together cornstarch and one egg. Beat into tomato mixture.
3. Let cool and then shape into a loaf or roll. Refrigerate until stiff.
4. Slice into 1/4" slices. Beat remaining egg. Dip slices into egg and then into cracker crumbs.
5. Sauté in butter or margarine until delicately browned.

—Mabel Haverstick, Viv's Varieties

Sweetened Sautéed Tomatoes and Cheese
Makes 6 servings

5 firm, ripe tomatoes
1/2 cup flour
3 Tbsp. brown sugar
salt to taste
pepper to taste
1/2 cup cheese, grated

1. Cut tomatoes about 1/2" thick. Pat slices in flour.
2. Sauté in hot oil, seasoning with sugar, salt, and pepper.
3. Place on a large platter and dot with grated cheese.
4. Cover with foil to melt cheese.

—Elva E. Martin, Rudy Breighner

◆

Sautéd Tomatoes with Herbs

tomatoes (as many as desired)
1 egg, beaten
basil to taste
oregano to taste
celery to taste
onion to taste
cracker crumbs
butter or margarine

1. Peel tomatoes. Slice about 3/8" thick.
2. Add seasonings to beaten egg.
3. Dip each slice into beaten egg and then into cracker crumbs.
4. Sauté in butter on both sides.

—Edith Groff, Groff's Homegrown Produce

Summer's Bounty: Zucchini-Tomato Gratin

Makes 6 servings

4 zucchini (about 1 1/2 lbs.), approx. 6" long
3 large, ripe tomatoes, approx. 1 1/2 lbs.
kosher salt
fresh ground pepper
3 Tbsp. Parmesan cheese, grated
fresh oregano leaves, or 1 tsp. dried oregano
1/4 cup olive oil

1. Slice zucchini into 1/2" thick slices. Slice tomatoes into 1/4" slices.
2. Place zucchini and tomatoes in a 9x13 baking dish, alternating slices.
3. Sprinkle with salt, pepper, cheese, and oregano. Drizzle with olive oil.
4. Bake at 400° for 35 minutes.

—Regine Ibold, Regine's Coffee

Market Rules, 1889

• Stalls outside, on the northern side of the Market House, are set apart for the sale of Fresh Fish, during market house only; and it shall be unlawful to sell fresh fish anywhere else in the market limits.
• The West King Street curb and the southwest angles of Centre Square are set apart for the sale of meat in not less quanitites than by the quarter.

MEATLESS MAIN DISHES

Orechielle with
Olives, Vegetables, and Mozzarella

Makes 4 servings

3 Tbsp. olive oil
2 medium zucchini, washed and cut into 1/2" cubes
1/2 tsp. salt
1/2 tsp. fresh ground pepper
8 oz. orechielle pasta
1 Tbsp. salt
1 cup black olives, pitted and chopped
4 ripe plum tomatoes, halved and diced
1 cup Parmesan cheese, grated
fresh ground pepper
8 oz. whole milk (fresh) mozzarella, cut in 1/2" cubes

1. Sauté zucchini in oil over medium heat, for about 5 minutes.
2. Stir in 1/2 tsp. salt and pepper. Drain zucchini into a large bowl.
3. Cook pasta in water with 1 Tbsp. salt, for about 10 minutes. Drain well.
4. Mix pasta and zucchini together.
5. Set oven to 375°. Grease a 9x13 baking dish.
6. Stir olives, tomatoes, and 1/2 cup Parmesan cheese into zucchini-pasta mixture. Add fresh ground pepper to taste.
7. Spoon into baking dish and sprinkle with mozzarella cheese cubes.
8. Bake for 10-12 minutes, until cheese is melted.
9. Serve with remaining Parmesan cheese.

—*Regine Ibold, Regine's Coffee*

Remedy to Prevent a Cold

garlic   sugar
white vinegar   dill pickle pieces
salt   spices

Some of our customers tell us that they eat 1 to 4 garlic cloves a day—or a mixture of the above—and they haven't had a cold since they started this regimen.

—*Scot Sturtevant, Pennsylvania Pickle Company*

Pasta Pultanesca
with Cooked Tomato Sauce

Makes 4 servings

3 Tbsp. olive oil
1 medium onion, chopped
1 can anchovies, packed in oil
2 cups basic homemade tomato sauce, or 2 cups plum tomatoes,
    canned and crushed
36 black olives, pitted and chopped
3 Tbsp. capers, drained and rinsed
1 cup Italian flat-leaf parsley, stemmed and coarsely chopped
1/2 cup fresh oregano leaves, or 1 Tbsp. dried oregano
1 bunch fresh basil, or 1 Tbsp. dried basil
1/2 tsp. red pepper flakes
1 lb. spaghetti noodles
1/4 lb. Parmesan cheese, grated

1. In a skillet, heat onion in oil until it is soft. Add anchovies and mash them
with a wooden spoon. Add tomato sauce, olives, herbs, and pepper flakes.
Simmer.
2. Cook spaghetti until firm to the bite. Add about 1/2 cup of pasta cooking
water to tomato sauce.
3. Divide most of sauce into 4 servings bowls. Top with spaghetti and then
top with remaining sauce. Serve with Parmesan cheese.

—Regine Ibold, Regine's Coffee

Summer Garden Pasta Sauce

Makes 4-6 servings

11/2-2 lbs. fresh plum tomatoes, coarsely chopped
1 medium onion, chopped
10 green or black olives, chopped
1/2 cup fresh parsley, minced
3 Tbsp. fresh basil, minced
4 tsp. capers
1/2 tsp. paprika
1/2 tsp. dried oregano
11/4 Tbsp. red wine vinegar
1/2 cup olive oil
1 lb. cooked pasta, preferably tomato-basil fettucini

1. Mix tomatoes, onion, olives, parsley, basil, capers, paprika, and oregano
together. Add vinegar and oil. Mix. Refrigerate overnight.
2. One hour before serving, allow mixture to come to room temperature.
3. Cook pasta. Combine pasta with other ingredients and serve.

—Connie Butto, The Herb Shop

Pasta with Asparagus
Makes 6-8 servings

2 lb. fresh asparagus, cut in 1" pieces
1 lb. thin spaghetti
8 slices bacon, cut in 1" pieces, or 2 Tbsp. vegetable oil
1/2 cup spring onions, sliced
1/2 tsp. black pepper
1/4 cup butter or margarine, melted
1/2 cup light cream
1/2-3/4 cup Parmesan cheese, grated

1. Cook asparagus in boiling salt water for 3 minutes. Drain. Set aside.
2. Cook spaghetti according to package directions. Drain. Return to kettle to keep warm.
3. If using bacon, fry until crisp. Sauté onion in bacon drippings until soft.
4. If not using bacon, sauté onion in 2 Tbsp. vegetable oil until soft.
5. Add asparagus and pepper. Heat.
6. Quickly toss spaghetti, asparagus mixture, butter, cream, and cheese together.
7. Serve immediately.

—Katie Fisher, Shreiner's Flowers

Asparagus Vegetable Bake
Makes 4-6 servings

5 potatoes
2 onions
2 cups asparagus
1/4 cup butter
1 tsp. salt
1/4 tsp. pepper
4 slices cheese

1. Slice potatoes. Place in a greased 2-qt. baking dish.
2. Dice onions and place on top of potatoes.
3. Layer asparagus on top. Dot with butter. Season.
4. Cover dish and bake for 1-1 1/2 hours at 350°.
5. Cover with a layer of cheese before serving.

—Elva E. Martin, Rudy Breighner

◆

Deviled Eggs and Asparagus

Makes 8-10 servings

2 lbs. fresh asparagus
10 eggs, hard-boiled
4.25-oz. can deviled ham, optional
1 tsp. onion, grated
$1/2$ tsp. Worcestershire sauce
$3/4$ tsp. dry mustard
1 tsp. cream
pepper to taste

1. Wash asparagus. Cut in 1" lengths, using only tender portions of stalk.
Cook in boiling water until just tender, adding tips during the last few
minutes of cooking. Drain.
2. Slice eggs in half lengthwise. Remove yolks.
3. Mash yolks. Blend with remaining ingredients. Stuff egg whites with
this mixture.
4. Put asparagus in bottom of shallow greased casserole dish.
5. Arrange deviled eggs on top. Pour cheese sauce over casserole.

Cheese sauce:
6 Tbsp. butter
6 Tbsp. flour
3 cups milk
$1/4$ tsp. dry mustard
1 tsp. salt
dash of pepper
2 cups cheese, grated
2 cups cornflakes
2 Tbsp. butter, melted

1. Melt 6 Tbsp. butter. Add flour and stir well.
2. Gradually add milk over low heat, stirring constantly until thickened.
Cook about 5 minutes longer over low heat.
3. Add seasonings and cheese. Stir until cheese is melted. Pour over casserole.
4. Crush cornflakes. Mix with 2 Tbsp. melted butter.
5. Sprinkle cornflake crumbs over top of casserole.
6. Bake at 350° for 15-20 minutes.

—*Mary Ellen Campbell, Baskets of Central Market*

Luscious Lancaster Tomatoes, Pasta-Filled

Makes 6 servings

6 large tomatoes
1/4 lb. capellini or orzo
1/4 cup fresh parsley, chopped
1 garlic clove, minced
1/4 cup fresh basil, chopped, or 1/2 tsp. dried oregano
salt to taste
pepper to taste
1/4 cup olive oil
1/4 cup Parmesan or Romano cheese

1. Cut off tomato tops. Spoon out seeds and cut away pulp. Chop pulp finely.
2. Salt interior of tomatoes.
3. Turn tomatoes over and allow them to drain for about 30 minutes.
4. Cook pasta al dente and drain well.
5. Mix pasta with parsley, garlic, and basil or oregano. Add salt and pepper if needed. Spoon mixture into tomatoes. Drizzle with olive oil and cheese.
6. Lightly oil a baking dish just large enough to hold the tomatoes.
7. Bake for 15 minutes at 350°, or until tomatoes have softened slightly.
8. Serve hot or at room temperature.

"I moved here 12 years ago, and wouldn't miss my weekly trip to market."
—Pat Golden, Central Market customer

Remedy for Sinus Relief

2 oz. fresh, grated, dry (no vinegar added) horseradish
juice of 1 or 2 lemons, depending on size

1. Mix horseradish with lemon juice until a moist consistency is reached.
2. Take 1/2 tsp. of mixture twice a day, between meals.

This remedy will effectively dissolve the mucous in the sinus cavities without damage to the membranes and will result in greater ease of breathing.

—Michael Long, Long's Horseradish

◆

Roasted Red Pepper Sauce with Sun-Dried Tomatoes

Makes 4-6 servings

6-oz. jar artichoke hearts, chopped
7-oz. jar roasted red peppers, chopped
1/4 cup fresh parsley, chopped
1/4-1/2 cup sun-dried tomatoes, minced
1/2 cup olive oil
1 Tbsp. red wine vinegar
1 clove garlic, minced
1/8 tsp. black pepper
1/4-1/2 cup black olives, chopped
1 lb. penne pasta, cooked

1. Combine all ingredients except pasta in large bowl and allow mixture to sit for half an hour, covered, at room temperature, so flavors develop.
2. Serve sauce either at room temperature or heated over hot penne.

—*Bonnie Sullivan, The Herb Shop*

Pasta Primavera

Makes 4 servings

8 oz. pasta
1 tsp. garlic, minced
1/2 cup olive oil
1/2 lb. mushrooms, sliced
2 small carrots, sliced
1 medium zucchini, thinly sliced
1 medium red pepper, seeded and thinly sliced
1 Tbsp. parsley, chopped
salt to taste
pepper to taste
Parmesan cheese, grated

1. Cook pasta according to directions.
2. While pasta cooks, sauté garlic in olive oil until lightly browned.
3. Add vegetables and stir. Sauté 3-5 minutes, or until tender, stirring frequently.
4. Toss vegetables and parsley with drained pasta.
5. Season with salt and pepper.
6. Serve with grated Parmesan cheese.

—*Melissa Nolt, S. Clyde Weaver, Inc.*

◆

Quick and Easy Vegetable Quiche

Makes 4-6 servings

2 cups sliced vegetables, parboiled: broccoli, carrots, asparagus,
    zucchini, etc.
1 cup shredded cheese, Swiss or cheddar
1 cup cottage cheese or ricotta cheese
3 eggs
1 cup milk
1/2 cup baking mix
salt to taste
pepper to taste

1. Place vegetables in a greased quiche dish or large pie plate. Sprinkle with
Swiss or cheddar cheese.
2. Mix cottage cheese, eggs, milk, baking mix, and seasonings in blender.
Pour over vegetables.
3. Bake at 350° for 30 minutes.

—Rose Meck, Robert S. Meck Produce

Spinach Soufflé

Makes 10 servings

2 cups (16 oz.) cottage cheese
3 eggs, beaten
30 oz. frozen spinach, thawed and drained
1 1/2 cups cheddar cheese, shredded
1/2 tsp. salt
dash of nutmeg

1. In a large mixing bowl, combine cottage cheese and eggs. Add spinach,
1 1/4 cups cheddar cheese, salt, and nutmeg.
2. Spoon into a greased 12x7 1/2 baking dish.
3. Bake at 350° about 45 minutes, until set.
4. Remove from oven. Sprinkle remaining cheese on top. Let stand for 5
minutes.

—Roberta B. Peters, Pennsylvania Dutch Gifts

> When I was little, I used to visit Central Market with my parents.
> I always enjoyed stopping at Angie Collata's fresh fruit stand. Before
> leaving her stand, she never failed to give me a banana. So you see,
> my first memories of Central Market are good ones.
>
> *—Ann White, Sunflower Foundation*

◆

Cheese Soufflé

Makes 6 servings

3 Tbsp. butter
3 Tbsp. flour
1 cup milk
1 cup cheese, grated
3 eggs, separated
1/2 tsp. salt
1/8 tsp. paprika
2 tsp. onion, grated (optional)

1. Melt butter. Stir in flour. Add milk gradually to mixture over low heat. Stir continually until smooth and thickened.
2. Add cheese. Stir until melted.
3. Add beaten egg yolks, salt, paprika, and onion.
4. Beat egg whites until stiff and fold gently into mixture.
5. Place in a greased casserole and set casserole dish in a pan of water.
6. Bake at 375° for about 40 minutes. Serve immediately.

—*Sara Jane Wenger, Chet's Flower Garden*

Veggie Sub

Makes 1 serving

Italian steak or sub roll
butter to taste
green olives, sliced
black olives, sliced
banana peppers, chopped
onion, sliced and sautéed
green pepper, sliced and sautéed
fresh mushrooms, sliced and sautéed
lettuce, sliced finely
tomatoes, chopped
mozzarella cheese, grated
Italian salad dressing

1. Partially split roll (do not cut completely in half) and butter both sides. Grill lightly in frying pan, electric skillet, or under broiler.
2. Layer vegetables on each side of roll.
3. Top generously with mozzarella cheese.
4. Bake at 400° just until cheese melts, approximately 5-8 minutes.
5. Drizzle Italian salad dressing over top of sandwich.
6. Fold sandwich together. Serve.

—*Hilda M. Funk, Givant's Jewish Baked Goods*

◆

Tomato Pot Pie

Makes 4-6 servings

1 qt. stewed tomatoes or fresh tomatoes, sliced
1/4 cup green pepper, finely chopped
3 Tbsp. sugar
1 tsp. salt
1/8 tsp. pepper
2 Tbsp. butter
1 cup flour
1 1/2 tsp. baking powder
1/2 tsp salt
3 Tbsp. butter, at room temperature
1/2 cup sharp cheese, grated
1/2 cup milk

1. Place tomatoes in a 2-qt. baking dish.
2. Sprinkle with green pepper, sugar, 1 tsp. salt, and 1/8 tsp. pepper. Dot with 2 Tbsp. butter.
3. Sift flour with baking powder and salt. Cut in butter with pastry blender.
4. Stir in cheese and milk until well blended.
5. Drop by spoonfuls on top of tomatoes.
6. Bake at 450° for 20-25 minutes.

—*Mary Keeport Breighner, Rudy Breighner*

The New Era, Lancaster, Saturday, October 5, 1889

The Central Market, A City Edifice to be Proud Of
A fine example of the Romanesque Style of Architecture
which Reflects Credit on the Architect and Contractor.
Good Accommodations

The lighting of the building is partly obtained from numerous large windows on all sides, raised above the side stall, but mainly from small dormer windows on all sides scattered all about the roof, the effect of this arrangement being very pleasing. The floor, which has a general, easy slope from east to west, is of concrete and is admirably adapted to secure cleanliness, as it can easily be flushed with water from plugs placed at convenient points. This fine even floor, so easily cleaned will leave no excuse for a dirty, ill smelling market, a subject of much universal complaint . . . The architect has confined himself principally to the south front in the design, and expenditure for ornament, as most of the other parts of the building are so surrounded by buildings as not to be much seen. This elevation shows a tower upon each corner and a gable in the centre . . .

MEATS
AND
MEAT DISHES

Stir-Fry Chicken with Fresh Vegetables

Makes 4 servings

2 boneless, skinless chicken breasts

Chicken marinade:
1 Tbsp. soy sauce
1 Tbsp. cornstarch
1 Tbsp. water

carrots, celery, sugar peas, broccoli, onions, water chestnuts, etc.

Vegetable marinade:
1/2 cup chicken broth
1 Tbsp. soy sauce
1 Tbsp. cornstarch
1/2 tsp. sugar
1 Tbsp. water

5 Tbsp. vegetable oil

1. Slice chicken into thin strips.
2. Mix soy sauce, cornstarch, and water together. Marinate chicken in the mixture while you prepare the vegetables.
3. Wash and then slice vegetables for stir-frying.
4. Mix chicken broth, soy sauce, cornstarch, sugar, and water together. Add vegetables to this marinade.
5. In 2 tablespoons of hot oil, cook chicken approximately 5 minutes, until it is white and tender. Remove from pan and set aside.
6. With remaining oil, stir-fry vegetables until tender.
7. Add chicken and continue heating until warm.
8. Serve over a bed of fluffy rice.

—Dawn N. Meck, Robert S. Meck Produce

◆

Sweet and Spicy Broiled Chicken with Fresh Pineapple

Makes 4 servings

1 fresh pineapple
1 clove garlic, minced
1 Tbsp. olive oil
2 large, skinless, boneless chicken breasts, halved
1 tsp. paprika
8-oz. jar Shenk's Red Tomato Preserves *

1. Preheat broiler.
2. Remove leaves from pineapple. Cut pineapple into quarters, from top to bottom. Remove core and shell.
3. Place minced garlic in olive oil. Rub into both sides of the 4 chicken pieces.
4. Sprinkle both sides of each chicken piece with 1/4 teaspoon paprika.
5. Arrange 4 chicken and 4 pineapple pieces in the preheated broiling pan. Form two rows, alternating chicken and pineapple.
6. Open jar of Red Tomato Preserves and microwave on High for 50 seconds, until preserves liquify.
7. Spoon half of preserves over chicken and pineapple. Brush lightly to distribute evenly.
8. Broil for 10 minutes, about 5 to 6 inches from heat.
9. Turn chicken and pineapple over. Spoon on remaining preserves. Brush lightly to distribute.
10. Broil for 10 more minutes.
11. Serve with white rice.

—Janden Richards, Shenk's Cheese Co.

* *If you cannot shop on Central Market, substitute tomato sauce for Shenk's Red Tomato Preserves.*

Many market-goers once had favorite "wagon boys" whom they patronized regularly. Some people reserved a boy and his wagon when going into the market. If the boy was still waiting when the person was finished shopping, an extra tip was in order. Elderly shoppers often asked boys to carry their baskets through the market as they shopped. Those who could not be early birds but still wanted to get the proverbial worm made arrangements with boys to go to the market as early as possible and have the cream of the crop set aside until they arrived.

◆

Grilled Herbed Chicken
Makes 12-16 servings

1/2 cup olive oil
1/2 cup fresh lemon juice
1 tsp. Dijon mustard
4 cloves garlic, crushed
1/4 cup fresh parsley, chopped
1 Tbsp. fresh rosemary, chopped
1 Tbsp. fresh tarragon, chopped
1 Tbsp. fresh sage, chopped
1 Tbsp. fresh oregano, chopped
1 Tbsp. fresh chives, chopped
1/2 tsp. salt
dash of fresh pepper
8 large, boneless, skinless chicken breasts, halved

1. Combine all ingredients except chicken in shallow dish. Add chicken breasts and marinate at least 2 hours, or overnight.
2. Grill or broil chicken for 7 to 9 minutes on each side, brushing with left-over marinade.

—Gail Johnson, Slaymaker's Poultry

Summer Chicken with Peas
Makes 10 servings

1 lb. small new potatoes
2 1/2 lbs. chicken pieces or chicken tenders
6 Tbsp. butter
salt and pepper to taste
2 Tbsp. lemon juice
3 green onions, with tops, sliced
1 lb. fresh peas or frozen peas
1/4 cup parsley, chopped

1. Scrub potatoes and peel a strip around center.
2. Brown chicken and potatoes slowly in butter. Season with salt and pepper to taste.
3. Sprinkle chicken with lemon juice. Reduce heat and simmer 30 minutes.
4. Add chopped green onions to butter in skillet. Sprinkle peas and parsley over chicken and potatoes. Salt peas lightly.
5. Cover again and simmer 15 to 20 minutes or until tender.

—Joyce G. Slaymaker, Slaymaker's Poultry

Thai Chicken and Vegetables

Makes 4-6 servings

2 Tbsp. vegetable oil
1 tsp. five-spice powder
1/2 tsp. garlic powder
1/2 tsp. ground ginger
1/2 tsp. black pepper
1/2 tsp. cayenne
1 Tbsp. soy sauce
1/2 lb. boneless, skinless, chicken breasts, cut in pieces
1/2 cup chicken broth
3 tsp. curry powder
2 Tbsp. rice wine vinegar, or regular vinegar
14 oz. coconut milk
1/2 head broccoli
4-6 carrots
1 red pepper
1 can sliced water chestnuts

1. Heat vegetable oil in large skillet over medium high heat.
2. Stir in five-spice powder, garlic powder, ground ginger, black pepper, cayenne, and soy sauce. Blend well.
3. Add chicken. Stir and cook for 5-8 minutes, until coated with seasoning and lightly browned.
4. Add chicken broth, curry powder, vinegar and coconut milk. Stir and bring to a boil. Reduce heat and simmer uncovered for 10 minutes.
5. Chop broccoli, carrots, and red pepper. Add to skillet, along with water chestnuts.
6. Simmer 20 minutes, or until vegetables are tender. Serve immediately over rice.

—*Bonnie Sullivan, The Herb Shop*

As a very young teenager I sometimes helped my father at the D.M. Weaver Smoked Meat & Cheese stand. More regularly my place to help was at the Arcade Market (located where the Prince Street Parking Garage now stands) because it was less busy.

When I worked at Central Market, my father always gave me money at noontime so I could eat a good, warm meal at the restaurant which stood where the public restrooms are located now. My favorite meal was baked beef pie. A sign at the counter advised customers who added sugar to their iced tea to "stir like lightning." It was during the war—and sugar rationing! This was a lively, friendly place to eat with a counter, stools, and, I believe, three tables.

—*Sara Jane Wenger, Chet's Flower Garden*

Chicken Parisienne

Makes 6 servings

6 whole boned, skinned chicken breasts
10½-oz. can cream of mushroom soup
10½-oz. can cream of celery soup
½ cup white wine
salt to taste
pepper to taste
Parmesan cheese
slivered almonds

1. Split chicken breasts into halves and arrange in an oblong baking dish.
2. Mix soups, wine, salt, and pepper and pour over chicken.
3. Sprinkle with Parmesan cheese and slivered almonds.
4. Bake uncovered at 350° for 1-1½ hours.

—Bernie Englert, Paul's Seafood

Chicken Cheese Bake

Makes 4-6 servings

4 large chicken breasts, skinned and deboned
8 slices Swiss cheese, or any other cheese
10½ oz. can cream of chicken soup
½ cup water
2 cups seasoned stuffing mix, or bread filling prepared to your liking
⅓ cup margarine or butter, melted
paprika

1. Arrange chicken in a single layer in a greased 9x13 pan. Place cheese on top.
2. Mix soup and water and pour over cheese and chicken.
3. Cover with filling, and drizzle with margarine or butter. Sprinkle with paprika.
4. Bake uncovered at 350° for 1 hour.

—Joanne Warfel, S. Clyde Weaver, Inc.

◆

Party Chicken

Makes 6 servings

1/4 lb. chipped dried beef
3 chicken breasts, halved, skinned, and boned
6 bacon slices
1 pint sour cream
10 1/2-oz. can cream of mushroom soup

1. Spread dried beef over bottom of baking dish.
2. Wrap chicken in bacon strips.
3. Mix sour cream and soup together. Pour over chicken.
4. Bake uncovered at 275° for 3 hours.

—Bernie Englert, Paul's Seafood

Sweet 'n Sour Chicken

Makes 4-6 servings

8 oz. Russian dressing
1 env. dry onion soup mix
10 oz. apricot preserves
4 whole chicken breasts, halved or deboned

1. Combine dressing, soup mix, and preserves.
2. Place chicken in a well buttered, shallow baking dish. Pour sauce over chicken.
3. Bake at 350° for 1 1/4 hours. Baste several times while baking.

—Joyce G. Slaymaker, Slaymaker's Poultry

My son has been coming to Market with me since he was an infant. For a number of years we walked to Market with Ben riding in a sturdy red wagon. The wagon was a great stroller and provided plenty of room to bring home the groceries. People still remember us as the family with the wagon.

One of the charms of Market is seeing familiar faces each week. Over the years my son has made friends with many of the standholders and other customers. He can count on a hug and a treat from Viv at the flower stand and looks forward to seeing his friends at the candy stand. The fish mongers often allowed him to pet soft-shelled crabs, inspect the clams, or study particularly unusual fish in the case.

—Gail Johnson, customer at Sensenig's, Viv's Varieties, etc.

◆

Brawny Chicken

Makes 6 servings

1½ cups spicy tomato juice
1 tsp. red pepper
¼ tsp. dry mustard
1 bay leaf
4½ tsp. Worcestershire sauce
¾ cup cider vinegar
1 tsp. sugar
3 cloves garlic, minced
3 tsp. butter
2-3 lbs. chicken pieces
3 medium onions, cut in rings

1. Boil first nine ingredients together for 10 minutes. Cool slightly.
2. Arrange chicken in a shallow pan and marinate for at least 2 hours, or overnight.
3. Bake uncovered at 425° for 45 minutes to an hour. Turn chicken at least once and baste frequently.
4. Garnish with onions.

—Jenny Schumacher

Jacques' Grilled Tabasco Chicken

6 chicken legs (approx. 3½ lbs.)
1 Tbsp. soy sauce
1 Tbsp. ketchup
1 Tbsp. cider vinegar
1 Tbsp. Tabasco sauce

1. Trim off tips of drumsticks. Cut halfway through the joint between thigh and leg for even cooking.
2. Mix soy sauce, ketchup, vinegar, and Tabasco sauce together with a whisk.
3. Dip chicken in marinade.

To grill: Place skin-side down on hot rack of grill, about 10" from heat for 10 minutes. Turn and cook 10 more minutes. Turn again and cook 10 more minutes. Let cool for 5 minutes before servings.

To broil: Place skin-side up on cookie sheet lined with foil. Broil for 10-12 minutes. Turn and broil for 8-10 minutes more. Move tray so that chicken is 6-8" from heat and cook skin-side up for 12-14 minutes more.

—Regine Ibold, Regine's Coffee

◆

Soy Marinade
for Chicken or Turkey
Makes 6 servings

1/2 cup soy sauce
1/2 cup cooking sherry
2 cloves garlic
3 Tbsp. honey or sugar
1 tsp. ground ginger
1/4 cup oil
6 boneless chicken breasts or turkey fillets

1. Combine all ingredients except the meat in a blender or food processor.
2. Place meat in a plastic bag, just slightly wider than the meat pieces. Place bag in a baking pan to catch any drips or leaks.
3. Pour marinade into bag. Twist and tie bag tightly, pressing out as much air as possible.
4. Refrigerate for 4-5 hours.
5. Place meat on hot grill and baste frequently with marinade. Turn meat to prevent burning, grilling until no more pink is visible.

—Joyce G. Slaymaker, Slaymaker's Poultry

Basting Sauce for Grilled Chicken

1/4 cup butter, melted
1/4 cup cider vinegar
1/4 cup water
1 Tbsp. Worcestershire sauce
salt to taste
pepper to taste

1. Blend ingredients together.
2. Pour over chicken.
3. Baste every few minutes while broiling or grilling chicken.

—Joyce G. Slaymaker, Slaymaker's Poultry

Oven-Baked Chicken
(Subtle Variation on a Theme!)

Chicken is beloved in this part of the world. And fresh chickens are sold every market day on Central Market.

Variations of seasonings create quite different subtleties of flavor. These four family favorites offer similar, yet distinctly unique, ways to prepare poultry in the oven.

Oven-Baked Chicken, I

Makes 6 servings

2 Tbsp. margarine or shortening
1¹/2 cups flour
1 tsp. salt
¹/4 tsp. pepper
6 or 7 chicken pieces (legs or breasts)

1. Melt shortening in a shallow pan.
2. Put flour and seasonings in plastic bag, add chicken, and shake, coating each piece of chicken with flour mixture.
3. Place chicken in pan. Bake at 400° for 45 minutes.

—Joyce Slaymaker, Slaymaker's Poultry

Oven-Baked Chicken, II

Makes 6-8 servings

3¹/2-4 lbs. frying chicken, cut up
2 cups dried bread crumbs
1¹/2 tsp. salt
1¹/2 tsp. paprika
1 tsp. celery salt
1 tsp. onion salt or flakes
¹/4 tsp. black pepper
1 tsp. poultry seasoning
milk

1. Remove skin from chicken parts.
2. Mix together all dry ingredients.
3. Dip chicken pieces into milk and then coat with crumb mixture.
4. Place in lightly greased baking dish. Cover.
5. Bake at 375° for 45-60 minutes.

—Ruth Thomas, Thomas Produce

◆

Oven-Baked Chicken, III

Makes 4-5 servings

2¹/2-3 lbs. broiler-fryer chicken, cut up
¹/4 cup shortening
¹/4 cup butter
¹/2 cup flour
1 tsp. salt
1 tsp. paprika
¹/4 tsp. pepper

1. Heat oven to 425°.
2. Wash chicken and pat it dry.
2. In oven, melt shortening and butter in a 9x13 baking pan.
3. Mix flour, salt, paprika, and pepper.
4. Coat chicken pieces thoroughly with flour mixture. Place chicken skin side down in melted shortening.
5. Bake uncovered for 30 minutes.
6. Turn chicken. Bake 30 minutes, or until thickest pieces are tender.

—Anne F. Kreider, Viv's Varieties

Sticky Baked Chicken

Makes 10 servings

6 chicken legs
6 chicken thighs
flour
1 stick butter or margarine
¹/2 tsp. salt
¹/2 tsp. pepper
pinch of saffron

1. Wash chicken legs and thighs. While they are still wet, dip them into flour.
2. Melt butter or margarine in a large skillet, and add chicken.
3. Sprinkle salt, pepper, and saffron over chicken. Brown on both sides; then place legs and thighs in a roast pan, with all the drippings.
4. Bake at 325° for 1 hour.

"My mother made this chicken and her mother, too."

—Viv Hunt, Viv's Varieties

◆

Chicken with Fresh Herbs and 40 Cloves of Garlic

3½-lb. chicken
kosher salt to taste
2 sprigs fresh thyme
2 sprigs fresh rosemary
2 sprigs fresh sage
2 tender stalks celery, with leaves
2 sprigs flat-leaf parsley
40 cloves garlic, unpeeled
3 Tbsp. olive oil
fresh ground pepper
toasted slices of crumbly bread

1. Preheat over to 400°.
2. Salt chicken inside and out. Stuff chicken with half the thyme, rosemary, sage, and celery. Add parsley and 4 cloves of garlic.
3. Put remaining herbs and celery in oval earthenware or enamel pot, just large enough to hold chicken.
4. Add oil, salt, pepper, and remaining garlic cloves.
5. Roll chicken in oil to coat completely.
6. Cover pot and bake for 1¾ hours.
7. Place chicken on serving platter. Degrease cooking juices and pour into sauce boat. Serve chicken hot with garlic cloves squeezed onto slices of bread.
—*Regine Ibold, Regine's Coffee*

Baked Chicken Wings
Makes 24-30 servings

12-15 chicken wings
1 cup soy sauce
1 cup brown sugar, packed
½ cup butter or margarine
1 tsp. dry mustard
¾ cup water

1. Disjoint chicken wings, discarding bony tips. Arrange meaty wing parts in shallow baking pan.
2. Combine soy sauce, brown sugar, butter, mustard, and water. Heat until butter and sugar dissolve. Cool. Pour mixture over wings.
3. Marinate in refrigerator for 2 hours, turning occasionally.
4. Bake in marinade at 350° for 45 minutes, turning once and basting with marinade occasionally. Drain on paper towels and serve hot or cold.
—*Jim Hollenbach, Slaymaker's Poultry*

◆

Chicken Cordon Bleu

Makes 6 servings

Bread filling:
1/2 cup butter
1/2 cup celery, chopped
1/2 cup onion, chopped
2 eggs
1 1/2-2 cups milk
1 bag bread cubes

1. Melt butter. Sauté celery and onions in it until tender.
2. Beat eggs lightly. Stir milk into eggs.
3. Gently fold sautéed vegetables, and milk and egg mixture into bread cubes.

Chicken Cordon Blue:
1 lb. ham, chipped
bread filling
2 cups cooked chicken, deboned
1 cup cream of chicken soup
1/2 cup milk
1/2 lb. Swiss cheese, sliced

1. Layer ham, bread filling, and chicken in a 2-qt. casserole dish.
2. Blend soup and milk together until smooth and pour over layered ingredients. Place cheese on top.
3. Bake at 350° for 1 1/2 hours.

—*Lorraine Good, Eisenberger's Bakery*

Marbled Chicken

Makes 6-8 servings

1 chicken
salt to taste
pepper to taste
butter to taste
chicken broth
sliced lemon

1. Using only a small amount of water, boil chicken until it is very tender.
2. Season with salt, pepper, and butter.
3. With a sharp knife, chop meat finely, packing white and dark meat in alternate layers in small bowl.
4. Strain the broth over the chicken and press the meat down in the bowl.
5. When cold, cut in thin slices. Serve with sliced lemon.

—*Mabel Haverstick, Viv's Varieties*

Chicken Newberg

Makes 10 servings

1/4 cup margarine
1 cup milk
1 cup heavy cream
10 1/2-oz. can cream of mushroom soup
1/2 cup cheddar cheese, grated
1/3 cup sherry
1-lb. pkg. frozen peas
3 cups cooked chicken, cubed
1/4 cup pimiento strips
10 patty shells

1. Melt margarine. Stir in milk, cream, and condensed soup.
2. Bring to a slow boil. Stir in cheese until melted.
3. Slowly mix in sherry and peas. Simmer for 20 minutes.
4. Fold chicken and pimento strips into sauce. Heat thoroughly.
5. Serve in patty shells.

—Joyce G. Slaymaker, Slaymaker's Poultry

Chicken a la King Supreme

Makes 6-8 servings

2 Tbsp. butter
1 tsp. onion, minced
1/2 cup flour
3 1/2 cups chicken stock
10 1/2-oz. can cream of mushroom soup
8 oz. cream cheese
3 cups diced, cooked chicken
1/4 tsp. pepper
2 hard-boiled eggs, diced
parsley
1 1/2 tsp. salt
1/4 tsp. pepper
12 frozen puff pastry shells

1. Melt butter. Add onion and cook slightly.
2. Add flour and blend to smooth into a paste.
3. Add chicken stock and cook to thicken mixture.
4. Add mushroom soup, cream cheese, and chicken. Simmer slowly, stirring to melt cream cheese.
5. Add diced eggs and parsley and season to taste. Serve over pastry shells.

—Ethel Stoner, John R. Stoner Produce

◆

Chicken in a Cloud

Makes 6-8 servings

Potato shell:
3¹/2 cups hot mashed potatoes, with no butter, milk or seasoning added
1¹/2 cups (6 oz.) cheddar cheese, shredded
2.8-oz. can french fried onions
2 Tbsp. chopped fresh parsley
salt to taste

Filling:
1¹/2 cups cubed, cooked chicken or turkey
10 oz. frozen mixed vegetables, thawed and drained (fresh vegetables
    may be substituted)
10¹/2-oz. can cream of chicken soup
¹/4 cup milk
¹/2 tsp. dry mustard
¹/4 tsp. garlic powder
¹/8 tsp. pepper

1. Combine potato shell ingredients. Spread over the bottom and up the
sides of a greased 2-qt. shallow baking dish.
2. In a large bowl, combine filling ingredients. Pour gently into shell.
3. Bake uncovered at 375° for 40 minutes. Let stand 5 minutes before
serving.

—Edith Groff, Groff's Homegrown Produce

Pan-Fried Turkey Steaks

Makes 4-6 servings

4-6 turkey breast fillets, cut ¹/2-³/4" thick
¹/4 cup flour
1 tsp. salt
¹/2 tsp. pepper
¹/2 tsp. onion powder
¹/2 tsp. celery salt
¹/4 cup butter or margarine

1. Coat turkey fillets with flour, salt, pepper, and herbs.
2. Preheat butter in skillet. Pan-fry over medium heat until done, about 5
minutes per side.

—Joyce G. Slaymaker, Slaymaker's Poultry

◆

Easy Turkey Parmigiana
Makes 4 servings

4 turkey breast fillets
1 egg, slightly beaten
1/2 cup bread crumbs
2 Tbsp. oil
1/4 cup onion, minced
1 cup tomato sauce or spaghetti sauce
4 oz. mozzarella cheese, sliced or shredded
grated Parmesan cheese (optional)

1. Dip turkey fillets into egg, and then into bread crumbs.
2. Brown slowly in oil.
3. Arrange fillets in a baking dish. Sprinkle onion on top and add tomato sauce.
4. Bake uncovered at 350° for 30 minutes.
5. Top with cheese and bake 10 minutes longer.

—Joyce G. Slaymaker, Slaymaker's Poultry

French Butter Roasted Cornish Game Hens
Makes 4 servings

4 fresh Cornish game hens
salt to taste
pepper to taste
1 medium onion, quartered
2 tsp. tarragon
1 Tbsp. fresh parsley, chopped
1 tsp. thyme
4 Tbsp. cold butter
4 Tbsp. melted butter

1. Remove giblets. Season hens inside and out with salt and pepper.
2. Place one quarter of onion and equal amounts of mixed herbs in each hen cavity, along with 1 Tbsp. cold butter in each bird.
3. Tie legs together and fold wings back. Baste hens with melted butter.
4. Cook in preheated 400° oven for 45 minutes, basting with butter at 10-minute intervals.

—Joyce G. Slaymaker, Slaymaker's Poultry

◆

Crepe Manicotti with Sausage
Makes 8 servings

Crepe Batter:
1 cup flour
1/2 tsp. salt
2 cups milk
3 medium eggs, beaten
2 Tbsp. butter, melted

1. Combine flour and salt.
2. Combine milk and eggs.
3. Slowly add liquid mixture to dry ingredients, using a whisk.
4. Allow batter to rest for 30 minutes, then add butter.
5. Stir batter before making each crepe.
6. Using a 2-oz. ladle, drop batter by ladle-fuls into frying pan. When one side is browned, flip crepe over to other side.
7. Stack crepes on a cookie sheet, with paper towels between the crepes.

Filling:
2 lbs. Ricotta cheese, or a combination of Ricotta and cottage cheese
1 lb. loose turkey sausage, browned and cooked
2 eggs, slightly beaten
1/4 cup parsley, chopped
salt
pepper
16 oz. tomato sauce
1/2 cup mix of Parmesan and Romano cheese, grated
1 cup mozzarella, grated

1. Combine all filling ingredients, except tomato sauce and grated cheeses. Blend well.
2. Stuff each crepe with filling.
3. Pour a layer of tomato sauce into a baking pan. Place stuffed crepes in pan.
4. Top with remaining tomato sauce.
5. Sprinkle with grated cheeses.
4. Bake at 350° for 35-40 minutes.

—Pamela Rohrer, Sensenig's Gourmet Turkey

For many years a lady came to the market that everyone called "The Peanut Lady." She had a distinctive appearance—socks and shoes that didn't match, very rosy cheeks, lots of makeup, and a hat that included a collection of peanuts and other things hanging on it.

—Ethel Stoner, John R. Stoner Produce

Sausage-Pinto Bean-Pasta Toss

Makes 4-6 servings

2 medium onions, chopped
1 medium green pepper, chopped
olive oil
3/4-1 lb. fat-free sweet or hot turkey sausage, cut in thick slices
15 oz. pinto beans, drained
8 oz. tomato sauce
2 tsp. oregano
garlic to taste
hot sauce to taste (optional)
8-12 oz. rotini pasta, cooked

1. Sauté onions and green peppers in olive oil over medium heat.
2. Add sausage and cook until browned.
3. Cover the pan and steam sausage until cooked, about 8-10 minutes, lifting lid occasionally to release moisture.
4. Add beans, tomato sauce, oregano, garlic powder, and hot sauce. Sauté until thoroughly heated, about 6-8 minutes.
5. In a large bowl, pour over cooked pasta and toss.

—*Pamela Rohrer, Sensenig's Gourmet Turkey*

Sausage Stew

Makes 4-6 servings

1 1/2 lbs. country-style sausage, cut in 1"-chunks
1 onion, diced
2 celery ribs, diced
water to cover
10 1/2-oz. can cream of celery soup
4-6 medium potatoes, peeled and quartered
2 cups frozen or fresh sliced carrots
2 cups frozen or fresh green beans

1. Brown sausage chunks with onion and celery.
2. Add water, cream of celery soup, potatoes, and vegetables. Cover and simmer until potatoes are soft. (If you use frozen vegetables, you may want to add them a bit later.)

Variation: For a tomato taste, use cream of tomato soup in place of celery soup.

"I remember my mother cooked sausage and potatoes together and served a vegetable on the side. I always enjoyed that meal! To make a one-dish meal, I cook the vegetables in the same pot and add the soup for a rich flavor."

—*Joyce Denlinger, S. Clyde Weaver, Inc.*

◆

Sausage in All Its Many Forms

As we travel and read more—and as foods from many traditions become more available to all of us—we discover two things—that despite our backgrounds, we share many similar foods, but we often use quite different names for them. Take sausages, for example.

"Sausage" is the English term for ground meat that has been stuffed in a casing. A comparable word in German is "wurst"; in Spanish, "chorizo"; and in French "andouille." Louisiana Creoles use the French term to describe their particular style of sausage—but it is considerably spicier than the original French type. The same can be said of chorizo. If a recipe is of Central or South American origin, the chorizo needs to be spicy. A Castillian recipe, on the other hand, requires chorizo that is mild and made with a lot of paprika.

In Lancaster County, sausage names can be very confusing. Many early settlers were from German-speaking countries, and Germany has a vast variety of wursts. When you hear the term "sausage" in Lancaster County, all you can be sure of is that the speaker is referring to some kind of wurst that is uncooked and needs to be fried, grilled, or baked. (American wursts that are cooked and ready to eat are typically called lunchmeat or carry a specific name such as liverwurst.) In Lancaster County and southeastern Pennsylvania, the predominant types of available sausages are fresh sausage, breakfast links, bockwurst, bratwurst, and Italian sausage. "Fresh" sausage is a general term; the meat is usually seasoned with salt and pepper only. When the mixture is put into a small casing, it is called breakfast sausage. In supermarkets they often bring in sausage from the "outside," and it is made with sage in the seasoning mix. Generally, the use of sage in sausage is more accepted south of the Mason-Dixon line.

A Willow Street butcher, named Sam Hippey (S.W. Hippey Meats), strongly influenced Lancaster County sausage. Sam seasoned his sausages with more than the standard salt and pepper. He added coriander, mace, nutmeg, and extra white pepper. He taught Lancaster about "bratwurst," but he never used the name. Generally, bratwurst are seasoned with salt, pepper, and a variety of herbs, depending on the "home" of the original recipe. There are probably as many bratwurst recipes in Germany as there are villages. One common characteristic of these sausages is their size. Bratwurst are usually linked in five- to six-inch pieces. Bratwurst are best when grilled and served with kraut and caramelized onions.

"Bockwurst" are predominately veal sausages that were traditionally made only during Easter season in Lancaster County. They are seasoned with parsley, egg, cracker crumbs, coriander, and pepper. Usually this variety is mild and the meat is very finely chopped, giving the sausage a white color. Consequently, bockwurst is sometimes called "weisswurst" or, in upper New York state, "white hots." A Lancaster County bockwurst has more white pepper than is standard in New York City but not nearly as much as a white hot. Presently, most bockwurst are made with pork, although our German sausagemaker uses 80% veal. Due to the high perishability of its ingredients, this sausage is usually steamed immediately when it is made and should be held frozen.

Mild Italian sausage is made with a variety of herbs and usually contains fennel or sometimes anise, which gives a sweet impression. Hot Italian sausage does not contain fennel but has paprika for color and cayenne pepper for "heat."

Another variety of sausage available in Lancaster County during the Easter holiday season is fresh "kielbasa" (garlic sausage). Most people know kielbasa as a smoked sausage, but this fresh variety is unique and worth a sampling when available. Traditionally, this sausage is eaten with horseradish. "Saucisson" is of French origin and often includes pistachios and plenty of garlic.

Many sausages are available in smoked versions. Smoking usually helps to preserve sausage, because the meat is cured and then smoked. The smoking process cooks the meat and also makes it drier. For this reason, many of today's poultry sausages are smoked, or at least frozen, due to the perishability of their meat base.

The pleasure of cooking with sausage is that the meat can be used in a host of creative ways. Although many traditional recipes use sausage in whole-link form, sausage can be cut into chunks and can give great flavoring to casseroles or single-pot dishes. Leftover grilled sausages are excellent in cold, mixed-rice salads. Paella without the spiciness and aroma of choriza takes on a different character, but other sausages can be substituted to create a more personal dish. Chinese-style stir-fried dishes can be adapted to include sausage instead of traditional meat.

As sausage-makers are limited only by their imaginations, the home cook is equally free to experiment and dream. Sausage provides many opportunities to spice up any menu.

—*Sam Neff, S. Clyde Weaver, Inc.*

◆

White Bean and Turkey Sausage Rigatoni

Makes 4 servings

8 oz. rigatoni pasta (5 cups)
8 oz. fully-cooked Sensenig's 98% fat-free kielbasa
half of a 10-oz. pkg. frozen spinach, thawed
29-oz. can low sodium stewed tomatoes
15-oz. can great Northern beans, rinsed and drained
3 oz. tomato paste
1/4 cup dry red wine or reduced sodium chicken broth
1 1/2 tsp. Italian seasoning, crushed
1/4 cup Parmesan cheese, shredded or grated

1. In a large saucepan prepare pasta according to package directions. Drain and return to pan.
2. Slice turkey kielbasa diagonally into 3/4"-pieces.
3. Drain thawed spinach well.
4. Add kielbasa spinach, tomatoes, beans, tomato paste, wine or chicken broth, and Italian seasoning to the cooked pasta. Stir to mix.
5. Spoon mixture into 4 ungreased casserole dishes or one 2-qt. casserole dish. Sprinkle with cheese.
6. Bake uncovered at 375° for 15-20 minutes (25-30 minutes for a 2-qt. casserole) or till bubbly and hot.

Note: To make in advance, do not sprinkle cheese on top. Cover with plastic wrap. Chill overnight. Remove plastic wrap. Bake, covered with foil, in a 375° oven for 45 minutes (55 minutes for a 2-qt. casserole) or until hot. Top with cheese.

A customer of Sensenig's Gourmet Turkey

Remedy for Stained Hands

rhubarb stalks, crushed   ripe tomato

Use either of these to wash extremely stained hands. Tomatoes are great for removing stains that come from working in the garden. Simply crush or mash rhubarb stalks or tomatoes in your hands and work on the stained area. Then wash your hands as usual.

—*Ethel Stoner, John R. Stoner Produce*

◆

Bratwurst with Apples and Onions
Makes 4 servings

1 Tbsp. butter
1 Tbsp. vegetable oil
6 bratwurst
1 apple, thinly sliced
1 onion, thinly sliced
2 Tbsp. flour
1½ cups chicken broth
1 Tbsp. vinegar
1 Tbsp. honey

1. In a frying pan, heat butter and vegetable oil. Add bratwurst and cook until brown.
2. Remove bratwurst and set aside.
3. Place apple and onion in pan. Sauté until lightly browned. Add flour. Mix well.
4. Add chicken broth, vinegar, and honey. Stir until mixture boils. Simmer for 5 minutes.
5. Return bratwurst to pan and simmer for 5 more minutes.

—Christine Weiss, German Deli

Bockwurst with Curry Sauce

1-2 bockwurst per person

Sauce for 1-2 Bockwurst
(multiply sauce ingredients by the number of persons at your table!)

1 small onion
¼ cup tomato puree
¼ cup ketchup
4 Tbsp. curry powder (to taste)

1. Sauté onions. When onions are soft, add puree, ketchup, and curry powder.
2. Add bockwurst and brown lightly.

—Sam Neff, S. Clyde Weaver, Inc.

◆

Bratwurst with Carmelized Onions

1½-2 bratwurst per person

Carmelized Onions (Sauce for 6 bratwurst)

6 large yellow onions
1 Tbsp. butter

1. Peel, halve, and slice onions.
2. Place onions in skillet with butter. Cover and steam for 5-10 minutes.
3. Remove cover, reduce heat, and simmer for 2-3 hours, stirring occasionally. Liquid will eventually evaporate and onions will brown to a golden color.
4. Remove onions. Add bratwurst (and additional butter if needed) and brown lightly.

—*Sam Neff, S. Clyde Weaver, Inc.*

Sausage Cheese Strata

Makes 6 servings

1 lb. fresh bulk sausage or smoked ham cubes
3 bagels (onion, garlic, or plain)
1 large onion, sliced
½ lb. extra sharp cheese, shredded
1 cup Cooper sharp cheese, shredded
6 large eggs
4 cups whole milk
1 cup light cream
1 tsp. salt
½ tsp. pepper

1. Sauté sausage in a frying pan until well browned. Drain on paper towels.
2. Chop sausage into small pieces.
3. With bagel lying flat on a cutting board, slice downward with a sharp knife to form thin, round coin shapes.
4. Layer bagel slices, onions, sausage, and cheese in a greased 2-qt. square casserole dish.
5. Whip together eggs, milk, cream, salt, and pepper.
6. Pour mixture over casserole ingredients and cover. Refrigerate for 24 hours.
7. Allow casserole to reach room temperature.
8. Bake at 350° for about 1 hour, or until brown and puffed in center.
9. Let stand for 10 minutes and serve.

—*Gray Sellers, Lancaster Bagel Company & Lancaster Citrus Company*

♦

Onion, Pepper, and Sausage Sandwich
Makes 6 servings

2 large green peppers
2 medium onions
1 tsp. salt
1/4 tsp. pepper
1 Tbsp. olive oil
6 4-oz. sweet Italian sausage patties
6 bagels (onion, garlic, seeded, or plain)

1. Sliver peppers into small strips, about 2" long.
2. Slice onions into thin rings.
3. Place peppers, onions, salt, and pepper into microwave dish. Add olive oil and process on High for 3 minutes. (The vegetables and seasonings can also be sautéed on top of stove.)
4. Broil, fry, or grill the sausage patties.
5. Cut bagels in half and toast. Place a sausage patty on half of each bagel. Top each with warm, green pepper and onion mixture and bagel half.
   —*Gray Sellers, Lancaster Bagel Company & Lancaster Citrus Company*

Beef Barbeque
Makes 6 servings

1/2 lb. sausage
1 1/2 lbs. hamburger
1 cup celery, diced
1 large onion, diced
12 oz. bottled chili sauce
1 1/2 cups water
8 oz. tomato sauce
1 1/2 Tbsp. prepared mustard
1 tsp. celery salt
1/4 tsp. pepper

1. Sauté sausage for 5 minutes. Remove from pan and set aside. Leave 1 Tbsp. drippings in the pan.
2. Brown hamburger. Add celery and onions and sauté.
3. Return sausage to pan. Stir in remaining ingredients.
4. Simmer for 45 minutes.
5. Serve in rolls, or over noodles or rice.
   —*Laura Hollenbach, Slaymaker's Poultry*

◆

Stuffed Burger Bundles

Makes 5 servings

1 pkg. bread stuffing
1/3 cup evaporated milk
1 lb. ground beef
1 cup condensed cream of mushroom soup
2 tsp. Worcestershire sauce
1 Tbsp. ketchup

1. Prepare stuffing according to package instructions.
2. Combine evaporated milk and meat.
3. Make 5 hamburger patties, each about 6" in diameter.
4. Put 1/4 cup stuffing in center of each.
5. Draw meat over stuffing and seal.
6. Place in greased 1 1/2-qt. casserole dish.
7. Combine remaining ingredients. Pour over patties.
8. Bake uncovered for 35-40 minutes at 350°.
—Hilda M. Funk, Givant's Jewish Baked Goods

Cheddar-Filled Beef Rolls

Makes 6 servings

1 1/2 lbs. lean ground beef
1/4 cup dry bread crumbs
2 Tbsp. barbeque sauce
1 egg
1/2 tsp. salt
1 cup cheddar cheese, shredded
1/4 cup dry bread crumbs
1/4 cup green pepper, chopped
2 Tbsp. water

1. Combine meat, bread crumbs, barbeque sauce, egg, and salt. Mix well.
2. Pat meat mixture into 14x8 rectangle on foil or waxed paper.
3. Combine cheese, bread crumbs, green pepper, and water. Pat cheese mixture over meat.
4. Roll meat jelly-roll fashion, beginning at narrow end.
5. Chill several hours overnight.
6. Slice into 6 servings. Lay in shallow baking pan.
7. Bake at 350° for 25 to 30 minutes.
—Dorothy Nolt, Chet's Flower Garden

Mrs. Burle's Special Burgers
Makes 4-6 servings

1 lb. lean ground beef
1 lb. ground turkey, from thigh
1 lb. lean German-style bratwurst, removed from casing
1 large onion, chopped
2 Tbsp. olive oil
salt
freshly ground pepper
large handful flat-leaf parsley, finely chopped
large handful lovage or celery leaves, finely chopped
large handful marjoram, finely chopped
large handful chives, finely chopped

1. Combine meats and onion with olive oil, salt and pepper.
2. Add herbs.
3. Shape into 6-oz. burgers. Grill on a charcoal grill until no longer pink inside.

These are also good cold!

—*Regine Ibold, Regine's Coffee*

Beef Pot Pie
Makes 4-6 servings

6 large potatoes, peeled and quartered
6 cups water
1½ lbs. ground beef
6 celery stems, chopped
small pinch saffron
1½ tsp. salt
dash of pepper (optional)
2 cups water
½ bag pot pie bow noodles

1. Cook first 7 ingredients together until potatoes are soft.
2. Add 2 cups water and bring to a boil.
3. Add pot pie bow noodles and cook an additional 15 minutes. Serve.
   —*Anna Marie Groff, Anna Marie Groff's Fresh Cut Flowers*

◆

Pudding—Scrapple—Mush

The Pennsylvania Dutch are well known for a wide variety of cured and cooked meats that trace their origins to Germany. As the German settlers altered the names of these foods, first into the local dialect of Pennsylvania Dutch, and then over time into English, many of these names became "ferhuddled" (mixed-up). One family of foods that causes major confusion in nomenclature are the cooked broth and meat mixtures called "puddin's."

One hallmark of the early Pennsylvania Dutch was their frugality. The Dutch subscribed to the admonition: "Waste not, want not." Most families raised their own meat and then butchered in the cool autumn months. After they took the prime cuts, the bones and trimmings remained. They used the best of the trimmings to make sausage. Then they cooked and picked the bones to make a rich broth. This was the first step in making "puddin's." After stewing a hearty broth, they added the meat trimmings back into the broth. And each family or community developed recipes for what else could be mixed in. This often included liver, heart, and kidney meat. The puddings were seasoned with salt and pepper and slowly cooked to a thick consistency. At this point in the process the options multiplied.

Many households ladled hot pudding meat into a crock and stored it for the winter in a cool cellar. Since a substantial portion of the ingredients was pork, there was often a fair amount of lard or fat in the mixture. As the pudding cooled, the fat rose to the top and formed a protective seal for the meat below. When it came time to use the meat, the cook removed the lard (for other uses).

Heated pudding is traditionally served over toast, pancakes, or waffles. Some people like to use fresh ground horseradish as a condiment with hot pudding. Others eat it with ketchup or chopped fresh onions.

Ring pudding is closely related to pan pudding. The primary difference is that ring pudding is stuffed into two- or three-inch diameter casings and stored in a refrigerator, rather than in a pan or crock in the cellar. Generally, ring pudding has more liver than pan pudding and is quite perishable.

When pudding meat is slowly cooked with a variety of flours and then chilled in a pan it is called "scrapple." Home cooks traditionally make scrapple with roasted cornmeal. Many butchers use a blend of cornmeal, wheat flour, and buckwheat flour.

Scrapple is customarily seasoned with salt, pepper, and a bit of thyme and/or oregano. Sometimes a bit of sage seasoning is used, but this is more Philadelphia in style than Lancastrian. Scrapple made with a high proportion of cornmeal has a yellow appearance, while a greater amount of buckwheat yields a grey color. Cornmeal gives a granular texture. Buckwheat is smoother, and if too much is used can make the result rather gummy.

Scrapple is prepared by cutting one-half inch thick slices from the chilled loaf. The slices are pan-fried until golden brown and crispy on both sides. Lancaster County cooks serve scrapple with apple butter or syrup. Traditionally, scrapple is a breakfast food and is often served on the menu with eggs.

"Pannhas" is a term sometimes used to refer to scrapple, but, technically, it is cornmeal that is cooked in a clear meat broth. Pannhas does not have any pieces of meat.

"Mush" is related to this family of food, but it contains no meat or meat broth. Mush is plain cornmeal cooked with water, and then chilled in a pan or mold. After the mush is cooled, it can be sliced and fried or steamed. Like scrapple, mush is frequently served as a breakfast food, often topped with pancake syrup. Mush is also similar to Italian polenta—although it would be shocking to a hungry Pennsylvania Dutch person, to eat mush with a salad or main dish.

—*Sam Neff, S. Clyde Weaver, Inc.*

Scrapple

1 lb. pudding meat or loose sausage
salt and pepper to taste
1 qt. water or pork broth
1½ cups cornmeal
¼ cup buckwheat flour

1. Stir meat and seasonings into boiling water or broth.
2. When mixture returns to a boil, slowly stir in the cornmeal and buckwheat flour. Stir constantly until thickened. Cover and simmer over low heat for 15 minutes.
3. Pour into 2 1-lb. loaf pans. Cool thoroughly; then refrigerate.
4. When scrapple is set, cut in ½" slices and fry in hot greased skillet, until both sides are browned and crusty.
5. Serve hot with ketchup, syrup, or apple butter.

◆

All-at-Once Spaghetti
Makes 5 servings

1 Tbsp. cooking oil
1 large onion, chopped
1/2 lb. ground chuck
1 1/2 tsp. salt
pepper to taste
16 oz. tomato sauce
1 1/2 cups water
1/4 lb. uncooked spaghetti
grated cheese

1. Heat oil in saucepan or skillet. Add onion and cook until soft.
2. Crumble in beef. Stir-fry until meat loses red color. Sprinkle with salt and pepper.
3. Pour in tomato sauce and water. Bring to a boil.
4. Break spaghetti in half or into smaller pieces. Sprinkle in a little at a time, stirring it into the sauce and keeping it separated.
5. Cover tightly and simmer 20-30 minutes. Stir often. Serve with cheese.
—Joyce Plasterer, Pennsylvania Dutch Gifts

"For Sauerkraut Lovers"
Makes 4 servings

1 large can sauerkraut
1-1 1/2 lbs. ground beef, unsalted

1. Mix meat with kraut. Bake at 350° for 1 hour.
—Anna Marie Groff, Anna Marie Groff's Fresh Cut Flowers

Ground Turkey Meatballs with Sweet and Sour Sauce
Makes 4-6 servings

Meatballs:
1 lb. ground turkey
1/2 cup onion, finely chopped
1/4 cup celery, finely chopped
1/4 cup fine dry bread crumbs
1 egg, beaten
1 Tbsp. soy sauce
1/2 teaspoon fresh grated ginger root, or a dash of ground ginger

1. Combine all ingredients. Shape into small balls, 3/4 to 1" in diameter. Place on jelly roll pan.
2. Bake at 400° for 15 minutes or until done.

Sweet and Sour Sauce:
8 oz. crushed pineapple
1/4 cup brown sugar
3 Tbsp. cider vinegar
2 tsp. cornstarch
2 tsp. Dijon mustard

1. Combine all ingredients. Cook and stir until thickened.
2. Combine with cooked meatballs.

—Joyce G. Slaymaker, Slaymaker's Poultry

Sweet and Sour Meatballs
Makes 8-12 servings

Meatballs:
2 lbs. ground beef
11/2 cups applesauce
1 tsp. salt
1/4 tsp. pepper to taste
1 cup cornflake crumbs
1 onion, chopped

Mix together and shape into meatballs.

Sweet and Sour Sauce:
1 cup ketchup
1 cup water

1. Combine sauce ingredients. Pour over meatballs.
2. Bake uncovered at 400° for 1 hour.

—Carol Simon, Baskets of Central Market

The West End Market, the smallest and most recent of the markets, began in 1954 in a building that had been a car dealership. The building at the corner of Lemon and Mary Streets ceased to be a farmers market in 1985 but is still occupied by a grocery store.

◆

Savory Chili

Makes 6 servings

1 medium onion, coarsely chopped
6 medium carrots, peeled, halved lengthwise, and chopped
2 Tbsp. oil
2 tsp. chili powder
1 tsp. ground cumin
1 tsp. marjoram or oregano
1/4 tsp. red pepper flakes
2 lbs. lean meat, cut into 1/2" cubes
2 Tbsp. oil
28 oz. crushed tomatoes
1 1/2 cups beef or chicken broth
2 Tbsp. lemon juice
1/4 cup tomato paste
14 1/2-oz. can kidney beans
3 cups cooked rice or barley (optional)

1. Cook onions and carrots in oil for 5 minutes.
2. Add chili powder, cumin, marjoram, and red pepper flakes. Set aside.
3. Brown meat cubes in oil on high heat. Add tomatoes, broth, lemon juice, and tomato paste.
4. Simmer until meat is tender.
5. Combine vegetable-meat mixture and kidney beans. Simmer for ten minutes.
6. Serve hot chili in bowls over rice or barley, if desired.

—Sara Jane Wenger, Chet's Flower Garden

"Red Hot" Turkey Chili

A reduced-fat chili con carne

Makes 6 servings

1 Tbsp. olive oil
1 large onion, diced
1 clove garlic, minced
1 lb. ground turkey breast meat
28 oz. crushed tomatoes
9-oz. jar Shenk's "Red Hot" Pepper Relish *
2 cups water
1 Tbsp. chili powder
1/2 tsp. basil
1 bay leaf
1/2 lb. (about 2 cups) dried kidney beans,
    which have been soaked overnight

1. Use a large, heavy pot with a tight-fitting lid. Sauté onion and garlic in olive oil.
2. Add ground turkey and brown it.
3. Add remaining ingredients and bring to a boil.
4. Cover, reduce heat, and simmer for 2½ hours, or until kidney beans are soft, stirring occasionally.

"This is a favorite Saturday evening meal. It slowly simmers on the stove as we go about our chores in the afternoon, sending a wonderful "home cooking" fragrance throughout the house. There's always enough to feed any last-minute visitors...just serve it over rice. Chili improves with age, so save leftovers for a middle-of-the-week meal when you don't feel like cooking."
— *Janden Richards, Shenk's Cheese Co.*

* If you are not able to shop on Central Market, substitute with 1 cup pepper relish, as hot or mild as you like it.

Simplified Cincinnati Chili
Makes 6-8 servings

1½ lbs. lean ground beef
2 cups onion, chopped
2 large garlic cloves, minced
1 Tbsp. chili powder
¼ tsp. ground cinnamon
dash of ground cloves
4 cups spicy vegetable juice
2 tsp. cocoa
2 16-oz. cans kidney beans, drained
grated cheese
chopped onion

1. Cook ground beef, onion, and garlic in a 6-qt. kettle over medium heat until browned and tender. Stir with a wooden spoon to break up meat and prevent it from sticking to the pan.
2. Mix in chili powder, cinnamon, and cloves. Cook briefly. Stir in vegetable juice and cocoa and heat to boiling.
3. Cover and reduce to simmer for 30-60 minutes.
4. Stir in beans and simmer for 15 more minutes.
5. Serve on top of hot spaghetti, with grated cheddar or Colby cheese on top. Garnish with chopped onion.

— *Regine Ibold, Regine's Coffee*

◆

Mike's Favorite Chili
Makes 10-12 servings

1½ medium onions, chopped
1 medium red pepper, chopped
1 small garlic clove, minced
2 jalapeno peppers, chopped
3 Tbsp. cooking oil
4 lbs. ground beef
8 Tbsp. chili powder
1 Tbsp. cumin
1 Tbsp. Tabasco
2 tsp. garlic salt
8 oz. beer
salt to taste
pepper to taste
1¼ cups water
8 oz. tomato sauce
4 oz. canned green chilies
14½-oz. can stewed tomatoes
1 bay leaf
canned kidney beans, to taste (optional)

1. Sauté onions, pepper, garlic, and jalapeno peppers in oil.
2. Add ground beef. Sauté until it loses its redness.
3. Add chili powder, cumin, Tabasco, garlic salt, beer, salt, and pepper. Let stand 2 minutes.
4. Add remaining ingredients. Simmer, covered, on low heat for 3 hours.
5. Remove bay leaf before serving. Serve with corn muffins.

—*Mike Manderewicz, Givant's Jewish Baked Goods*

◆

Barbequed London Broil

Makes 4 servings

3/4 cup Italian-style salad dressing
1 tsp. Worcestershire sauce
1 tsp. dry mustard
1/4 tsp. thyme
1 medium onion, sliced
2 Tbsp. butter or margarine, melted
1 1/2 lbs. flank steak, scored, or top round, scored

1. Combine all ingredients except steak.
2. Place steak in a shallow dish and pour marinade over top. Cover and refrigerate at least 4 hours, or overnight.
3. Remove steak from marinade. Grill over hot coals for 5 minutes on each side. Occasionally brush marinade over top. Steak may also be broiled in oven, 3-4" from heat for 5-7 minutes on each side.
4. Onions from marinade may be sautéed in skillet over hot coals or on top of stove for about 3 minutes.
5. To serve, slice steak in thin, diagonal slices across the grain. Sprinkle onions on top.

—Mike Bell, M.E. Bell, Inc.

Barbequed Steak Roll-Ups

Makes 4 servings

1/2 cup cooking oil
1/4 cup lemon juice
1 Tbsp. paprika
2 tsp. Worcestershire sauce
dash of Tabasco sauce
2 Tbsp. vinegar
2 tsp. sugar
2 cloves garlic, crushed
1 1/2 lbs. sirloin tip steak (boneless) or top round steak
mushroom caps or cherry tomatoes

1. Combine first 8 ingredients in a screw-top jar and shake vigorously to mix.
2. Cut steak into 1"x2 1/2" pieces. Pound pieces with a mallet. Place in marinade and refrigerate 1 hour.
3. Remove from marinade. Wrap meat around mushroom caps or cherry tomatoes. Fasten with large wooden toothpicks or wooden skewers.
4. Grill over medium coals 12-15 minutes, turning once or twice until done.

—Mike Bell, M.E. Bell, Inc.

◆

Pot Roast in Foil

Makes 8-10 servings

4 lbs. beef pot roast
1 env. dry onion soup mix
10 1/2-oz. can cream of mushroom soup

1. Place an 18"x30" piece of heavy duty aluminum foil in a 9x13 baking pan. Place meat on foil.
2. Sprinkle onion soup mix over top of meat. Spread meat with mushroom soup.
3. Fold foil over meat and seal securely.
4. Roast at 300° for 4 hours.

—*Ann F. Kreider, Viv's Varieties*

Bacon-Liver Bake

Makes 4 servings

6 slices bacon, chopped
1 cup onion, chopped
1/4 cup flour
1 tsp. salt
dash of pepper
1 lb. beef liver, cut in serving-size pieces
1 1/2 cups milk
1/4 cup fine dry bread crumbs
1 Tbsp. margarine, melted

1. In skillet, combine bacon and onion. Cook till bacon is crisp and onion is tender. Remove, reserving drippings in skillet.
2. Combine flour, salt, and pepper. Coat liver with flour mixture.
3. Brown liver in bacon drippings. Remove liver and place in a greased 10x6 baking dish.
4. Blend reserved flour mixture with drippings in skillet until smooth. Add milk.
5. Cook and stir till thickened and bubbly. Pour sauce over liver. Sprinkle bacon and onion over all.
6. Combine crumbs and melted margarine. Sprinkle on top of liver mixture.
7. Bake uncovered at 350° for 25 minutes. Garnish with parsley and serve.

—*Ernie Thomas, C. H. Thomas Meats*

Easy Barbequed Pork Chops

Makes 6 servings

6 pork chops, 1" thick
salt to taste
8 oz. tomato paste
1/2 cup water
1/3 cup onion, finely chopped
1/4 cup extra hot ketchup
1 Tbsp. sugar
1 Tbsp. vinegar
1 Tbsp. Worcestershire sauce

1. Sprinkle salt on pork chops.
2. Grill over medium coals for 35 minutes, turning once.
3. Meanwhile, in a small saucepan, combine remaining ingredients and
bring to a boil. Reduce heat and simmer uncovered for 15 minutes.
4. Brush chops with sauce and grill 5 more minutes.

—Mike Bell, M.E. Bell, Inc.

Ham Loaf, I

Makes 16-20 servings

4 lbs. smoked ham, ground
6 lbs. fresh pork, ground
6 cups bread crumbs
4 cups milk
8 eggs
2 tsp. salt
1/2 cup onions, chopped (optional)

1. Mix ingredients well.
2. Form into 1 large loaf or 2 smaller loaves.
2. Bake large loaf at 350° for 2-21/2 hours. Bake smaller loaves for 1-11/2
hours.

—Florence Merkey, Shenk's Cheese Co.

◆

Ham Loaf, II

Makes 8-10 servings

2 beaten eggs
1/2 cup milk
1/2 cup crackers, finely crushed (approx. 14 saltines)
1/2 cup onion, finely chopped
1/2 tsp. dry mustard
1/8 tsp. pepper
2 lbs. Bell's own ground ham loaf mix*
1/2 cup packed brown sugar
2 Tbsp. orange or pineapple juice
2 Tbsp. vinegar
1/2 tsp. dry mustard
1/4 cup crushed pineapple (optional)

1. Combine eggs, milk, crushed crackers, onion, 1/2 tsp. dry mustard, and pepper.
2. Add ground meat. Mix well.
3. Shape into an 8"x4" loaf and place in a 9x13 baking pan.
4. Bake at 350° for 1 hour.
5. Combine brown sugar, fruit juice, vinegar, and 1/2 tsp. dry mustard. Add crushed pineapple, if desired.
6. Spoon glaze over loaf. Bake 20 minutes longer, basting occasionally with sauce.

—*Mike Bell, M.E. Bell, Inc.*

* *Note: If you are unable to shop on Central Market, substitute with 1 lb. fresh pork, ground, and 1 lb. smoked ham, ground.*

Aloe Vera Healing

Customers have reported astonishing results from using the healing qualities of this plant.

1. Sore throat: Peel off rough edges. Suck a chunk as you would a throat lozenge.
2. Burns: Squeeze juice from a puffy leaf. Usually this keeps blisters from forming.
3. Bites and rashes: Apply juice to reduce pain and itchiness.
4. Cuts: Apply juice to combat infections.
5. Dry scalp: Rub on scalp.

—*Sara Jane Wenger, Chet's Flower Garden*

Creamed Ham and Asparagus

Makes 4-6 servings

1 lb. fresh or frozen asparagus, cut in 1" pieces
1 Tbsp. cornstarch
1½ cups milk, divided
2 Tbsp. butter or margarine
1 tsp. salt
½ tsp. pepper
½ tsp. dried parsley flakes
1½ lbs. fully cooked ham, cubed
3 hard-boiled eggs, chopped
2 cups (8 oz.) cheddar cheese, shredded
toast or biscuits

1. In a saucepan, cook asparagus in a small amount of water until tender. Drain and set aside.
2. In a medium saucepan, mix cornstarch and 2 Tbsp. milk. Add butter, salt, pepper, and remaining milk. Cook and stir over medium heat until thickened and bubbly.
3. Add parsley, ham, eggs, cheese, and asparagus. Cook and stir over low heat until ham is warmed and cheese is melted.
4. Serve over toast or biscuits.

—*Verna Sauders, Kauffman's Fruit Farms*

Turkey Ham Burgers

Makes 6 servings

3/4 lb. boiled ham, turkey ham, or 12-oz. can of Spam
½ lb. cheese (your choice)
1 small onion
3 Tbsp. ketchup
3 Tbsp. milk
2 Tbsp. mayonnaise
2 Tbsp. pickle relish

1. Grind meat, cheese, and onion through food chopper. Mix thoroughly.
2. Add ketchup, milk, mayonnaise, and pickle relish.
3. Spread on open-faced rolls and place under broiler until lightly browned.

—*Katie Fisher, Shreiner's Flowers*

◆

Salmon Salad Sandwiches

Makes 4 servings

3-oz. pkg. cream cheese
1 Tbsp. mayonnaise
1 Tbsp. lemon juice
1 tsp. dill seed
1/4 tsp. salt
dash of pepper
6-oz. can pink salmon, drained, with skin and bones removed
1/2 cup carrots, shredded
1/2 cup celery, chopped
4 sandwich rolls

1. In a mixing bowl, beat cream cheese and mayonnaise together.
2. Add lemon juice and seasonings.
3. Gently mix in salmon and vegetables.
4. Pile lightly in rolls.

—*Mary S. King, Shreiner's Flowers*

Stewed Kidneys

Makes 6 servings

2 beef or pork kidneys
1 Tbsp. butter
1 Tbsp. flour
1/2 pint stock or boiling water
1 Tbsp. Worcestershire sauce
1 Tbsp. mushroom ketchup
salt to taste
pepper to taste
4 Tbsp. sherry

1. Be sure kidneys are perfectly fresh. Split kidneys in half. Trim off sinews and fat.
2. Cut kidneys in small pieces. Place in a pot. Cover with cold water.
3. Place pot on medium heat and bring almost to boiling.
4. Drain water. Cover with fresh cold water and heat again. Do this three times, being careful that water never boils.
5. Brown butter in a frying pan.
6. Add flour and stock or boiling water. Stir until mixture boils.
7. Add Worcestershire sauce, mushroom ketchup, salt, and pepper.
8. Add kidneys. Stir again until thoroughly heated.
9. Remove from stove. Add sherry and serve immediately.

—*Mabel Haverstick, Viv's Varieties*

◆

Lemon Shrimp and Pasta

Makes 4 servings

2 Tbsp. olive oil
2 garlic cloves, crushed
1 Tbsp. fresh thyme, chopped
zest of 1 lemon
juice of 2 lemons
ground black pepper
20 jumbo shrimp, peeled and de-veined, with tails on
2 Tbsp. olive oil
1 Tbsp. butter
2 cloves garlic, crushed
the white part of 2 large leeks, thoroughly washed and
    cut into julienne strips
2 tomatoes, seeded and chopped
juice of 1 lemon
8-12 oz. pasta, cooked and drained

1. Mix together 2 Tbsp. olive oil, 2 garlic cloves, thyme, lemon zest, juice of 2 lemons and pepper.
2. Marinate shrimp in refrigerator in this mixture for 3 hours; then marinate at room temperature for 45 minutes.
3. In a skillet over medium heat, melt together 2 Tbsp. olive oil, 1 Tbsp. butter, and remaining 2 cloves crushed garlic. Add leeks. Cook on low heat, stirring often until leeks are caramelized.
4. Stir in tomatoes and heat briefly. Increase heat to a high setting.
5. Add shrimp and marinade. Sauté quickly, just until shrimp turn opaque. Remove from heat.
6. Add juice of one lemon. Toss with hot pasta. Serve immediately.

—Cindy Cover, Plum Street Gourmet

◆

Gotta-Have-It Garlic Shrimp

Makes 3-4 servings

1 lb. shrimp (in shells)
1/4 lb. butter
1 lemon
14.2-oz. bottle Pennsylvania Pickle Company's "Gotta Have It"
   Garlic Lover's Sauce*

1. Spread half of shrimp in a baking dish.
2. Cover shrimp with "Gotta Have It" sauce.
3. Slice butter into 1/4" pieces. Slice lemon into thin slices.
4. Layer butter and lemon slices over shrimp and sauce. Place remaining shrimp on top.
5. Cover with foil and refrigerate for at least 2 hours, or overnight.
6. Preheat oven to 450°. Bake shrimp, covered, for 15 minutes.

—*Scot Sturtevant, Pennsylvania Pickle Company*

* *If you are unable to shop on Central Market, substitute cocktail sauce.*

Scalloped Scallops

Makes 4-6 servings

1 lb. scallops
2 Tbsp. margarine
2 large celery stems, chopped finely
3 scallions, chopped
1/2 lb. mushrooms, sliced
1 Tbsp. lemon juice
2 Tbsp. flour
1 1/4 cups milk
1/4 tsp. salt
dash of pepper
1/2 cup bread crumbs
1 Tbsp. margarine

1. Preheat oven to 400°.
2. Rinse and dry scallops.
3. Melt margarine in large frying pan. Sauté celery and scallions for 2-3 minutes. Add mushrooms and sauté vegetables for another 2 minutes.
4. Add scallops and lemon juice, stirring occasionally for another 3-4 minutes.
5. Sprinkle with flour, stirring until well blended.
6. Gradually add milk, salt, and pepper, stirring until mixture thickens.
7. Pour into casserole dish, cover with buttered crumbs, and bake 8-10 minutes.

—*Edna Martin, C.Z. Martin Sons*

◆

Captain Tom's Fish Bake
Makes 6 servings

1/2 cup celery, chopped
1 cup onion, chopped
1/2 cup parsley, chopped
2 lbs. fish fillets (flounder, haddock, etc.)
1 tsp. salt
1/8 tsp. pepper
1/4 cup vegetable oil
3/4 tsp. paprika
16 oz. tomato sauce

1. Combine celery, onion, and parsley. Layer in a large, shallow, greased baking dish.
2. Place fish in overlapping layers over the vegetables.
3. Season with salt and pepper. Drizzle oil over the top. Sprinkle with paprika.
4. Bake at 375° for 10 minutes. Pour the tomato sauce over the fish and bake 30-35 minutes longer, or until fish is flaky and sauce bubbles. Baste fish frequently with sauce.

—*Bernie Englert, Paul's Seafood*

Scalloped Oysters
Makes 4 servings

1 1/2 cups coarse cracker crumbs
8 Tbsp. butter, melted
1 pint oysters
1/2 tsp. salt
1/2 tsp. pepper
dash of nutmeg
2 Tbsp. parsley (optional), chopped
1/4 cup oyster liquid
2 Tbsp. milk

1. Combine cracker crumbs and butter. Put a thin layer of crumbs in the bottom of a baking dish.
2. Add half of oysters and one-third of remaining crumb mixture, sprinkling each layer with seasonings. Repeat.
3. Pour oyster liquid and milk over the casserole. Top with remaining crumbs.
4. Bake at 450° for 30 minutes.

—*Mrs. Martha Flory, C.Z. Martin Sons*

◆

Grandmother Weaver's Oyster Crackers

Makes 6-8 servings

12-16 oz. Table Water or Falcon Crackers (flat crackers, not too salty)
1 pint fresh oysters with liquid
2 Tbsp. butter
1/8 cup parsley, chopped (optional)
salt to taste
pepper to taste
3 cups milk, approximately

1. Break crackers in halves or thirds.
2. Layer crackers, oysters, butter, and parsley in a greased 2 1/2-3 qt. casserole dish. Add salt and pepper to each layer.
3. Fill casserole dish with milk.
4. Set aside for 2 hours.
5. Bake 1-1 1/2 hours at 350°.

"When Grandmother Weaver (Mrs. S. Clyde Weaver) had the family for dinner, this was one of her signature dishes, along with cooked dandelion and a myriad of other stuff. The big challenge is finding the correct cracker. Carr's Table Water crackers are good, but Grandmother prefers crackers a bit heavier and thicker. Experiment with what's available in your area."

—*Sam Neff, S. Clyde Weaver, Inc.*

Salmon Cakes

Makes 6-8 servings

1 can salmon
2 cups fresh bread crumbs
1/2 cup fresh onion, chopped
1/4 cup fresh celery, chopped
4 beaten eggs

1. Combine all ingredients.
2. Shape into cakes.
3. Sauté in shortening, turning a few times until both sides are browned.
—*Rose Meck, Robert S. Meck Produce*

CASSEROLES

◆

Chicken Divan
Makes 6-10 servings

2 10-oz. pkgs. frozen broccoli
2 cups cooked chicken, cut in small pieces
2 10½-oz. cans cream of chicken soup
1 cup mayonnaise
1 tsp. lemon juice
½ tsp. curry powder
½ cup cheddar cheese, grated
½ cup bread crumbs
1 Tbsp. melted margarine

1. Cook broccoli and place it in a greased glass baking dish. Place chicken on top of broccoli.
2. Mix soup, mayonnaise, lemon juice, and curry. Pour mixture over chicken.
3. Sprinkle cheese on top.
4. Mix crumbs and butter. Sprinkle on top of cheese.
5. Bake at 350° for 25 to 30 minutes, or until bubbly.

—Katie Stoltzfus, Eisenberger's Bakery

Crab-Cheese Soufflé
Makes 4 servings

6 slices bread, cubed
½ lb. cheddar cheese, cubed
1 small can sliced mushrooms or 1 cup fresh mushrooms, sliced
6-8 oz. crabmeat
3 eggs, well beaten
½ cup butter, melted
½ pint light cream or evaporated milk

1. Preheat oven to 350°.
2. In a 2-qt. casserole dish, layer bread, ¼ lb. cheese, mushrooms, crabmeat, and the remaining cheese.
3. Blend eggs and butter together. Add cream or milk to egg mixture.
4. Pour liquid over casserole ingredients.
5. Place casserole in a pan of water.
6. Bake for 1 hour at 350°.
7. Serve immediately.

—Mary Kay McMichael, Givant's Jewish Baked Goods

Tuna Cracker Casserole

Makes 4-6 servings

2 cups saltine crackers, broken
6-oz. can tuna
2 cups noodles, cooked
1 cup cheddar cheese, grated
10^1/$_2$-oz. can cream of mushroom soup

1. Layer half of crackers on the bottom of a 1^1/$_2$-2 qt. greased casserole dish.
2. Layer tuna on top. Follow with noodles and a second layer of crackers.
3. Sprinkle cheese on top.
4. Pour soup over the casserole.
5. Bake at 350° for 45 minutes.

—Ruth H. White, Chet's Flower Garden

Tuna Noodle Casserole

Makes 4-6 servings

8 oz. noodles
6-oz. can tuna
10^1/$_2$-oz. can cream of mushroom soup
1 cup milk
^{1}/$_2$ tsp. salt

1. Cook noodles. Drain and set aside.
2. Flake tuna in mixing bowl.
3. Add soup, milk, and salt.
4. Fold in cooked noodles. Place in a greased 1^1/$_2$-2-qt. baking dish.
5. Bake at 350° for 25 minutes.

—Sallie Lapp, Sunflower Foundation

We substitute at the Pennsylvania Dutch Gifts stand whenever Ron and Roberta, the owners, take a much-needed vacation. One day while I was attending to some tourist customers, a man shook my hand and said, "I know you!" It was a guide that took us on a bus tour from Boston to Nova Scotia two years ago. What a nice compliment to receive! Central Market is part of a small world.

—Parke and Joyce Plasterer

◆

Italian Supper

Makes 4-5 servings

1 lb. ground beef
1 medium onion, chopped
1/2 tsp. oregano
1 tsp. salt
1/3 cup water
10 1/2-oz. can condensed tomato soup
2 cups wide noodles, cooked
4 oz. sharp cheddar cheese, grated

1. Brown beef and onions. Add oregano and salt.
2. Add water to soup and then combine with meat.
3. Add noodles. Stir well.
4. Place in a 1 1/2-2-qt. greased casserole dish. Sprinkle with cheese.
5. Bake at 350° for 30 minutes.

—Ruth H. White, Sunflower Foundation

String Pie

Makes 6-8 servings

1 lb. ground beef
1/2 cup onion, chopped
1/4 cup green pepper, chopped
15 1/2-oz. jar spaghetti sauce
8 oz. spaghetti, cooked and drained
1/3 cup Parmesan cheese, grated
2 eggs, beaten
2 Tbsp. butter
1 cup cottage cheese
1/2 cup mozzarella cheese, shredded

1. Cook beef, onion, and green pepper in a large skillet until meat is browned. Drain.
2. Stir in spaghetti sauce. Mix well.
3. Combine spaghetti, Parmesan cheese, eggs, and butter in a large bowl. Mix well.
4. Grease 9x13 pan. Place spaghetti mixture along bottom and sides of pan.
5. Spread cottage cheese over top. Pour sauce mixture over cottage cheese. Sprinkle mozzarella cheese on top.
6. Bake at 350° for about 20 minutes.

—Ann White, Sunflower Foundation

Cheeseburger Pie

Makes 4-6 servings

1 lb. ground beef
1/2 cup onion, chopped
1 1/2 cups milk
3/4 cup baking mix
3 eggs
1/2 tsp. salt
1/4 tsp. pepper
2 tomatoes, sliced
1 cup cheddar cheese, shredded

1. Brown beef and onion. Drain. Spread in a greased 10" pie plate.
2. Beat milk, baking mix, eggs, salt, and pepper in a blender for 15 seconds.
3. Pour over beef.
4. Bake 25 minutes at 400°.
5. Top with tomatoes and cheese.
6. Bake 5-8 minutes longer.
7. Cool 5 minutes before serving.

—Kitty Longenecker, Givant's Jewish Baked Goods

Delicious One-Dish Dinner

Makes 6-8 servings

5 medium potatoes
6 carrots
1 medium onion
1 1/2 tsp. salt
1/2 tsp. pepper
butter
2 lbs. hamburger

1. Peel, wash, and slice potatoes and carrots.
2. Grease a 2-qt. casserole dish. Layer potatoes on the bottom.
3. Place a layer of carrots on top of potatoes.
4. Slice onion very finely and place on top of carrots.
5. Season with salt and pepper.
6. Place chunks of butter on top of casserole.
7. Make hamburger into patties. Place meat on top of onion and butter to completely cover the casserole.
8. Add one inch of water to casserole and cover with foil.
9. Bake at 350° for 1 1/2 hours.

—Mark Keeport Breighner, Rudy Breighner

◆

Six Layer Dinner
Makes 6-8 servings

1 Tbsp. butter
2 cups potatoes, sliced
2 cups carrots, sliced
2 cups frozen peas
1 large onion, thinly sliced
salt to taste
pepper to taste
1 cup celery, diced
1¹/2 lbs. ground beef, lightly browned
29-oz. can tomato sauce or 1 quart home-canned tomato sauce

1. Preheat oven to 350°.
2. Butter a 3-qt. casserole dish or roast pan. Layer vegetables and meat in order listed. Pour tomato sauce over casserole. Cover.
3. Bake for 1¹/2 hours.

—Mrs. Martha Flory, C. Z. Martin Sons

Zucchini Hamburger Bake
Makes 4-6 servings

1 lb. ground beef
6 cups zucchini, thinly sliced
¹/2 cup bottled barbeque sauce
¹/2 cup soft bread crumbs
¹/2 cup Parmesan cheese, grated

1. In a large skillet, brown ground beef and zucchini slices for about 7-10 minutes, or until slices are transparent. Stir frequently.
2. Pour barbeque sauce over meat and zucchini. Toss until well blended.
3. Sprinkle with bread crumbs and cheese.
4. Place skillet 5" from broiler and broil for 1-2 minutes or until crumbs are golden brown.

—Mabel Haverstick, Viv's Varieties

Hamburger Chow Mein
Makes 6-8 servings

1¹/2 lbs. hamburger
¹/2 cup onion, chopped
10¹/2-oz. can cream of mushroom soup

WE HAVE
STROEHMANS

BREAD

STOLTZFUS
BAKED GOODS

OUR SPE

CHOW

Fre

BLACK RAS

JAM

HOME
MADE
JELLY
1.75 8 OZ

RED
RASBERRY
JELLY

BLACK
RASBERRY
JAM
OR JELLY

◆

10¹/2-oz. can cream of chicken soup
3 cups water
1¹/2 cups celery, chopped
¹/2 cup uncooked rice
3 Tbsp. soy sauce
1 can chow mein noodles

1. Brown meat and onion.
2. Blend soups, water, celery, rice, and soy sauce with meat.
3. Bake in a 3-qt. casserole for 1¹/2 hours at 350°.
4. Stir, then sprinkle chow mein noodles on top. Bake 30 more minutes.

—Sara Jane Wenger, Chet's Flower Garden

Dried Beef Pasta Party

Makes 4-6 servings

¹/4 lb. dried beef, chopped fine
1 cup sharp cheddar cheese, grated
1 cup macaroni, uncooked
1¹/2 cups milk
10¹/2-oz. can cream of celery soup
1 small onion, chopped
1 hard-boiled egg, for garnish, if desired

1. Mix all ingredients except egg together in a greased 1¹/2 qt. casserole dish.
2. Bake at 350° for 1¹/2 hours.
3. Slice hard-boiled egg on top before serving, if desired.

—Lois Thomas, C. H. Thomas Meats

Hot Fruit Casserole

24-oz. jar chunky applesauce
20-oz. can pineapple chunks, drained
15-oz. can dark, sweet, pitted cherries
¹/4 cup walnuts
¹/2-³/4 cup brown sugar

1. Lightly grease a 9" baking dish. Put applesauce on bottom of dish.
2. Arrange pineapples and cherries in applesauce.
3. Top with walnuts and brown sugar.
4. Bake at 350° for 45 minutes. Remove from oven and stir while hot. Delicious with ham.

—Tina House

◆

Penny Casserole

Makes 6 servings

1¼ lbs. red potatoes, cubed
1 lb. smoked sausage, sliced, or 10 hot dogs, sliced
2 Tbsp. dried onion
1 cup frozen peas, thawed
10½-oz. can cream of celery soup
3 Tbsp. butter
1 Tbsp. prepared mustard
⅛ tsp. pepper

1. Cook potatoes in boiling salt water until tender. Drain.
2. In a greased 2½-quart baking dish, combine potatoes, sausage or hot dogs, onion, and peas.
3. Combine soup, butter, mustard, and pepper. Gently stir into potato-meat mixture.
4. Bake uncovered at 350° for 25 minutes or until thoroughly heated.

—Carol Martin Hottenstein, C.Z. Martin Sons

Pot Pie

Makes 8 servings

2½ cups flour
½ tsp. salt
1 Tbsp. shortening
2 eggs
¼-½ cup water
stock

1. Mix flour and salt.
2. Cut shortening into flour and salt.
3. Add beaten eggs and enough water to make a soft dough.
4. Roll out dough as thin as possible. Cut into 1" x 2" rectangles and drop into 2 quarts boiling vegetable, chicken, or beef stock.
5. Cook for about 20 minutes, or until pot pie is tender.

—Sallie Lapp, Sunflower Foundation

> The Fulton Market, located east of Frederick Street between Plum and Hand Streets in the northeastern part of town, was rather detached from the other Lancaster markets. The 1907 building originally had 150 standholders. When the market closed in 1971 there were only six stands. The building has since been occupied by several different businesses.

BREAKFASTS

◆

Hearty Breakfast Bake

Makes 12 servings

1 lb. chipped ham
1/4 lb. mushrooms, sliced
1/2 cup onion, chopped or sliced
small bunch of green onions with tops
2 medium tomatoes, chopped
2 cups mozzarella cheese, shredded (or your choice of cheese)
11/4 cups baking mix
12 eggs
1 cup milk
11/2 tsp. salt
1/2 tsp. pepper
1/2 tsp. oregano

1. Layer ham, mushrooms, onions, tomatoes, and cheese in order in a 9x13 baking pan.
2. Beat together remaining ingredients and pour over layered ingredients.
3. Bake at 350° until golden brown, about 30 minutes.

Variation: Dried mushrooms and dried tomatoes may be added. Bulk sausage (cooked and drained) may be used instead of ham.

—*Dorothy Nolt, Chet's Flower Garden*

The New Era, Lancaster, Saturday, October 5, 1889

The Central Market, A City Edifice to be Proud Of
A fine example of the Romanesque Style of Architecture
which Reflects Credit on the Architect and Contractor.
Good Accommodations

The floor plan of the building shows an admirable arrangement of stalls and aisles, with entrances on all sides of the edifice. The truckers and farmers are placed in the centre of the market, the butchers being along the walls and the fish stall at the outside of the rear of the building . . . The stalls which will be in place within two weeks will all be constructed in the most approved modern style, all being of yellow pine.

The butchers' blocks will be of oak . . . there will be 100 farmers' and truckers' stalls, 72 butchers' and 20 fish stalls, 252 altogether.

The small streets about the building will be put in good condition as soon as possible, and in a little while our people will have one of the finest market houses in the State and all at a total of $26,500 . . . the only regret is that it does not occupy a site where it could be seen to its fullest advantage . . .

◆

Overnight Eggs

Makes 8 servings

16 slices white bread
2 cups ham, cooked and cubed
1 cup cheese, grated
6 eggs
3 cups milk
1/2 tsp. salt
1/2 tsp. dry mustard
2 cups cornflakes, crushed
1/2 cup butter or margarine, melted

1. Grease a 9x13 baking pan. Cut crusts off 8 slices of bread, and place bread on bottom of pan. Sprinkle with cubed ham and grated cheese.
2. Cut crusts off remaining 8 slices of bread and lay bread over ham and cheese.
3. Beat eggs and milk. Add salt and dry mustard.
4. Pour over bread, ham, and cheese.
5. Mix cornflakes with melted butter. Sprinkle over top.
6. Cover with foil and refrigerate overnight.
7. Bake uncovered at 350° for 1 hour.

—Joyce Plasterer, Pennsylvania Dutch Gifts

Sheepherder's Breakfast

Makes 10 servings

1 lb. sliced bacon
1 medium onion, chopped
4 cups hash brown potatoes
10 eggs
salt to taste
pepper to taste
2 cups cheddar cheese, shredded (optional)
fresh parsley, chopped, to garnish

1. In a large skillet, cook bacon and onion until bacon is crisp. Drain bacon and onion. Remove all but 1/2 cup of bacon drippings.
2. Add hash browns to skillet. Mix well.
3. Cook over medium heat for 10 minutes, turning when browned.
4. Make 10 "wells," evenly spaced in the hash browns. Place one egg in each well. Sprinkle with salt and pepper. Sprinkle with cheese, if desired.
5. Cover and cook over low heat for about 10 minutes, or until eggs are set.
6. Garnish with parsley and crumbled bacon. Serve immediately.

—Mary H. Harnish, Groff's Homegrown Produce

◆

Breakfast Ham Ring

Makes 8 servings

10 eggs
1 lb. ground, fully cooked ham
1 lb. bulk pork sausage
1½ cups soft bread crumbs
½ cup milk
2 Tbsp. dried parsley flakes
1 Tbsp. prepared horseradish (optional)

1. In a large bowl, lightly beat 2 eggs.
2. Add ham, sausage, bread crumbs, milk, parsley, and horseradish. Mix well.
3. Press into a greased 6-cup ring mold.
4. Bake at 350° for 1¼ hours.
5. Near the end of baking time, prepare scrambled eggs using remaining 8 eggs. Season as desired.
6. Remove ring from oven and drain juices. Unmold onto serving platter. Fill center with scrambled eggs. Serve immediately.
—*Joanne Warfel, S. Clyde Weaver, Inc.*

Eggs a la Goldenrod

Makes 8 servings

6 hard-boiled eggs
2 cups thin white sauce (see below)
salt to taste
pepper to taste
8 slices toast

1. Chop egg whites and combine with white sauce. Add salt and pepper.
2. Arrange slices of toast on a platter. Pour white sauce over toast.
3. Press egg yolks through a sieve. Sprinkle yolks lightly over top of toast.

White sauce:
3 Tbsp. butter or margarine
2 Tbsp. flour
1 tsp. salt
2 cups milk

1. Melt butter in a heavy saucepan or double boiler.
2. Add flour and salt. Stir well until blended.
3. Slowly add milk, stirring constantly until a smooth sauce is formed.
—*Anna Ruth Breckbill, Willow Valley Farm*

◆

Baked Eggs with Mushroom Sauce

Makes 6 servings

Baked Eggs:
butter or margarine
6 large eggs (or more)
3/4 cup Monterey Jack cheese, grated
mushroom sauce
fresh parsley, chopped

1. Preheat oven to 350°.
2. Heavily butter 6 muffin cups.
3. Break 1 egg into each cup. Bake about 8 minutes until egg whites are almost set.
4. Remove from oven. Top each egg with about 2 Tbsp. cheese. Bake 2 minutes more until cheese is melted.
5. Place eggs on a plate and top with mushroom sauce. Sprinkle with parsley.

Sauce:
1/2 lb. small mushrooms
3 Tbsp. butter or margarine
2 Tbsp. onion, chopped
1/2 cup chicken broth
1/2 cup heavy cream
1 tsp. cornstarch
dash of pepper
3 Tbsp. parsley, chopped

1. Wipe mushrooms with a damp paper towel.
2. Chop stems along with 8 caps to make 1 cup of chopped mushrooms. Quarter remaining caps.
3. Melt butter. Add onions and chopped mushrooms. Cook for 3-5 minutes until onion is soft.
4. Stir in broth. Add quartered mushroom caps. Sauté briefly.
5. Heat on high for 5 minutes.
6. Stir in cream and cornstarch. Stir in pepper and parsley.
7. Simmer for 3-5 minutes over moderate heat until thickened.
—*Laura Hollenbach, Slaymaker's Poultry*

As a boy, I went to Market early in the morning around 4 a.m. to help set up Dad's meat stand. Then around 6:30 a.m., my grandfather Elmer Thomas would take me down to the Queen Street Restaurant and buy me breakfast—two glazed doughnuts and a cup of hot chocolate. What a treat! This was the only time I got glazed doughnuts. That made getting up at 3:30 a.m. worth it.
—*Ernie Thomas, C.H. Thomas Meats*

◆

Old-Fashioned Waffles

Makes 4 servings

2 cups flour
1/2 tsp. baking soda
2 tsp. baking powder
1/2 tsp. salt
2 eggs, separated
2 cups buttermilk
1/4 cup butter, melted

1. Sift together flour, soda, baking powder, and salt.
2. In a separate bowl, beat egg whites.
3. Add buttermilk, butter, and egg yolks to flour mixture.
4. Fold in stiffly beaten egg whites.
5. Bake in a waffle iron.

—*Mary Ellen Campbell, Baskets of Central Market*

Granola

12 cups dry oatmeal
1 1/2 cups wheat germ
1 cup dry milk
1 cup brown sugar
1 cup coconut (optional)
1/2 cup sesame seeds (optional)
1 cup pecans, chopped (optional)
1 1/3 cups oil
1 1/3 cups honey
4 Tbsp. water
3 tsp. vanilla
2 cups raisins

1. Combine dry ingredients, except raisins. Combine oil, honey, water, and vanilla separately.
2. Combine dry mixture with liquid ingredients, leaving raisins aside. Mix well.
3. Bake in 2 large, shallow pans for 25-35 minutes at 300°. (Note: Granola may burn easily if glass pans are used.)
4. Mix in raisins after baking or add to individual serving bowls.

—*Joyce G. Slaymaker, Slaymaker's Poultry*

SAUCES, TOPPINGS, JAMS

◆

Roast Beef Sauce

Makes 6 servings

12-oz. jar home-style beef gravy
1/3 cup low-fat sour cream
3-4 Tbsp. prepared horseradish
1/4 cup sautéed onions or mushrooms (optional)

1. Blend all ingredients in a small saucepan. Heat, but do not boil.
2. Serve with roast beef.

—Michael Long, Long's Horseradish

Spicy Barbeque Sauce

Makes 5 servings

(This recipe is for 2 cups chopped turkey or pork.)

1 onion, chopped
1 stem celery, chopped
1/2 cup ketchup
1/4 cup brown sugar
2 Tbsp. vinegar
2 tsp. mustard
1 tsp. Worcestershire sauce

1. Combine all ingredients. Cook until celery and onion become soft.
2. Serve immediately over meat, or store in refrigerator until ready to use.

—Arlene Leaman, S. Clyde Weaver, Inc.

Raisin Sauce for Ham

Makes 2 cups

1/2 cup brown sugar
1 tsp. dry mustard
2 Tbsp. cornstarch
2 Tbsp. vinegar
2 Tbsp. lemon juice
1 1/2 cups water
1/2 cup raisins

1. Mix brown sugar, dry mustard, and cornstarch together.
2. Add remaining ingredients. Cook, stirring constantly, until thickened.
3. Serve over slices of cooked ham.

—Arlene Leaman, S. Clyde Weaver, Inc.

Tomato and Apple Butter Sauce

16-oz. can tomato sauce
1 cup apple butter
3 Tbsp. Worcestershire sauce
3 garlic cloves, finely chopped

1. Combine all ingredients together in saucepan. Simmer over medium heat for 3 minutes.
2. Brush over meat the last 5 minutes it cooks. This is great for pork or hamburgers.

—Mary Ellen Campbell, Baskets of Central Market

Balsamic Salad Dressing

2/3 cup pure olive oil
1/3 cup balsamic vinegar
1 Tbsp. shallots, finely chopped
1 Tbsp. fresh basil, finely chopped
1 tsp. sugar
salt to taste
pepper to taste

Combine all ingredients in a bowl. Chill. Serve over salad.

—Mary Ellen Campbell, Baskets of Central Market

Creamy Salad Dressing

Makes 1 pint

3 tsp. sugar
1/4 tsp. salt
1 tsp. celery seed
4 Tbsp. vegetable oil
1/4 tsp. onion salt
2 Tbsp. vinegar
6 Tbsp. mayonnaise

1. Mix ingredients together until smooth.
2. Serve over lettuce salad or other greens.

—Lena King, John R. Stoner Produce

◆

Honey Dijon Poppy Seed Dressing
Makes 1 cup

1/2 cup vegetable oil
1/2 cup honey
2 Tbsp. rice vinegar
1 tsp. poppy seeds
1 Tbsp. champagne mustard (or other prepared mustard)
1/4 tsp. salt

1. Combine all ingredients and mix well.
2. Toss with salad greens.

—Ethel Stoner, John R. Stoner Produce

Salad Dressing for Sandwiches
Makes 1 pint

14-oz. can condensed milk
1 tsp. prepared mustard
3/4 cup vinegar
2 eggs

1. Put all ingredients in a small mixing bowl. Beat until well blended.
2. Refrigerate.
Note: This dressing makes delicious ham or chicken salad.

—Dorothy W. Stauffer, Nye's Sandwich House

Croutons

leftover bread
butter
Italian herbs, or
Parmesan cheese, or
garlic powder, or
onion powder

1. Cut bread into small cubes.
2. Melt a stick of butter. Drizzle butter over bread cubes.
3. Add generously one of the above seasonings. Stir well.
4. Spread bread cubes on cookie sheet.
5. Bake at 275° for 10-15 minutes. Turn once.
6. Allow to cool. Serve in salads, soups, or as a snack. Freeze leftovers in plastic bags.

—Carole Manderewicz, Givant's Jewish Baked Goods

Mom's Smear Kaese

Makes 2¹/₂-3 qts. cheese spread

2 qts. milk
3-oz. block white American cheese, grated or sliced
4 oz. Velveeta cheese

1. Heat milk. Add cheese. Stir on low heat until cheese is melted.
2. Stir while cooling, so no crust forms. Cool. Spread on bread or crackers.
—Barbie King, Spring Glen Farm Kitchens, Inc.

Maple Syrup— as a Topping and Flavoring

1. Cook maple syrup down to the consistency of molasses and then serve it on vanilla or maple nut ice cream, lemon sherbet, rice pudding, or plain custard.
2. Fill the hollowed center of a grapefruit half with maple syrup; it's delicious.
3. Use maple syrup for sweetening in eggnog.
4. Add a tablespoon of maple syrup to a glass of milk; children love it.
5. Pour a little maple syrup over your favorite hot or cold cereal.
—Elton Moshier, Pure Maple Syrup

Strawberry Butter for Bread

¹/₂ cup softened butter
6 strawberries, finely chopped
2 Tbsp. powdered sugar
¹/₂ orange peel, grated

Cream all ingredients together. Spread on bread or rolls.
—Mary Ellen Campbell, Baskets of Central Market

Herb Butter for Bread

¹/₂ cup softened butter
1 Tbsp. milk
3 tsp. green onion, minced
¹/₂ tsp. dill
¹/₂ tsp. tarragon

Cream all ingredients together. Spread on bread or rolls.
—Mary Ellen Campbell, Baskets of Central Market

Maple Nut Frosting

1½ cups maple syrup
½ Tbsp. light corn syrup
2 egg whites
½ cup nut meats

1. Boil maple syrup and corn syrup to 240°, until it spins a thread when dropped from tip of spoon.
2. Beat egg whites until stiff. Add syrup slowly to the whites, beating constantly. Continue beating until mixture reaches a spreadable consistency.
3. Add broken nut meats just before spreading on the cake.

—Elton Moshier, Pure Maple Syrup

Caramel Frosting

Makes enough to frost a 9x13 cake

½ cup butter or margarine
1 cup brown sugar, packed
¼ cup milk
1¾-2 cups confectioners sugar, sifted

1. Melt butter in saucepan. Add brown sugar. Boil over low heat for 2 minutes, stirring constantly.
2. Add milk. Keep stirring until mixture boils. Remove from heat and cool.
3. Add confectioners sugar by half cups. Beat well after each addition, adding sugar until frosting is thick enough to spread.

Spiced Pear Jam

Makes 10-12 cups

8 cups (5½ lbs.) pears, peeled and chopped or ground
4 cups sugar
1 tsp. cinnamon
¼ tsp. ground cloves

1. Combine all ingredients in a large kettle.
2. Simmer uncovered for 1½ to 2 hours, or until thick, stirring occasionally. Stir more frequently as mixture thickens.
3. Remove from heat. Skim off foam.
4. Cool and spread on bread or rolls, or pour into sterile jars and seal.

—Lena King, John R. Stoner Produce

DESSERTS
AND
CANDIES

◆

Lemon Fruit Refreshment

Makes 6 servings

2 3-oz. pkgs. lemon gelatin
2 cups boiling water
64 small marshmallows
2 bananas, sliced
1 cup crushed pineapple, drained (reserve juice)

Topping:
1 egg, beaten
2 Tbsp. butter
2 Tbsp. flour
1 cup pineapple juice

1.3 oz. env. Dream Whip

1. Dissolve gelatin in 2 cups boiling waiter.
2. Dissolve marshmallows in hot gelatin. Allow to cool.
3. Add bananas and pineapple to gelatin.
4. Pour gelatin into 9x13 pan. Chill until firm.
5. Combine topping ingredients. Cook topping until thickened.
6. Add Dream Whip mix according to directions on box.
7. Fold into chilled gelatin.
8. Allow to set before serving.

—*Marty Stauffer, S. Clyde Weaver, Inc.*

Fruit Float

Makes 6 servings

16 oz. canned fruit, undrained
11-oz. can mandarin oranges, undrained
15¼-oz. can pineapple chunks, undrained
6 bananas, sliced
1 Tbsp. lemon juice
3.4-oz. pkg. instant lemon pudding

1. Combine all fruits and fruit juices.
2. Add lemon juice and instant pudding. Mix well.
3. Chill and serve.

Note: Fresh fruits, like apples, grapes, and peaches, may also be added.
—*Verna Sauders, Kauffman's Fruit Farms*

◆

Lemon Lush Dessert

Makes 12 servings

1/2 cup margarine, softened
1 cup flour
1/2 cup pecans, chopped
1 cup powdered sugar
8 oz. cream cheese
91/2 oz. whipped topping
2 3.4-oz. pkgs. instant lemon pudding
3 cups milk

1. Mix together margarine, flour, and pecans, reserving a few pecans for garnish.
2. Press into a 9x13 pan.
3. Bake for 15 minutes at 325°. Cool.
4. With a mixer, combine powdered sugar and cream cheese. Fold in 1 cup whipped topping.
5. Spread on top of baked mixture.
6. Mix together lemon pudding and milk. When thickened, spread over cream cheese mixture.
7. Spread remaining whipped topping over pudding. Sprinkle reserved nuts on top.
8. Refrigerate a few hours before serving.

—*Edna Martin, C.Z. Martin Sons*
—*Lois Thomas, C.H. Thomas Meats*

Tapioca Fruit Salad

Makes 8 servings

4 cups water
pinch of salt
1/3 cup minute tapioca
3-oz. pkg. fruit gelatin (your choice)
1/2 cup sugar
1 cup fruit (your choice)
whipped cream (optional)

1. Bring water to a boil.
2. Add salt and tapioca. Simmer for 3 minutes.
3. Remove from heat. Add gelatin and sugar. Stir while cooling.
4. When cool, add fruit and whipped cream, if desired.

—*Annie Jean Miller, Sunflower Foundation*

Lemon Tapioca

Makes 4 servings

4 Tbsp. instant tapioca
3/4 cup sugar
1/8 tsp. salt
2 cups water
1 tsp. fresh lemon juice, or lemon juice concentrate
1/2 cup cream, whipped, or 1 cup whipped topping

1. Place tapioca, sugar, salt, and water in a kettle. Bring to a full boil.
2. Remove from heat and stir in lemon juice. Allow to stand until cold.
3. Fold in whipped cream and serve.

—*Helen A. Thomas, Thomas Produce*

Tapioca Cream

Makes 4-5 servings

2 egg yolks, slightly beaten
2 cups milk
2 Tbsp. sugar
2 Tbsp. quick-cooking tapioca
1/4 tsp. salt
1 tsp. vanilla
2 egg whites
1/4 cup sugar
light cream or whipping cream

1. In a saucepan, combine egg yolks, milk, 2 Tbsp. sugar, tapioca, and salt over low heat, stirring constantly, until mixture boils.
2. Cool slightly and chill.
3. Stir vanilla into tapioca.
4. In a separate bowl, beat egg whites until foamy. Beat in 1/4 cup sugar, 1 Tbsp. at a time. Continue beating until stiff and glossy. Fold into tapioca mixture.
5. Serve cooled, topped with whipped cream.

—*Ann F. Kreider, Viv's Varieties*

Market Rules, 1889

• Dogs must be kept out of the Market House, and the owners of them will be held responsible for any violation of this rule.

Tapioca Pudding
Makes 12 servings

1/2 cup tapioca pearls
6 cups milk, scalded
2 eggs
1 cup sugar
1 tsp. vanilla
1/2 tsp. salt

1. Soak tapioca overnight in water to cover.
2. Add tapioca to scalded milk. Stir until clear over medium heat.
3. Beat eggs and sugar together. Add them to tapioca mixture, stirring constantly over medium heat. Continue stirring until tapioca is thickened.
4. Add vanilla and salt.
5. Cool before serving.

—*Becky Ann Esh, Esh's Deli*

Delicious Pudding
Makes 8 servings

1 cup brown sugar
3/4 cup water
4 Tbsp. butter
1 tsp. salt
1/2 tsp. baking soda
3/4 cup sugar
6 cups milk
4 egg yolks
3/4 cup flour
1 tsp. vanilla
8 oz. whipped topping

1. In a kettle, mix brown sugar, water, butter, salt, and baking soda together. Bring to a boil.
2. Add sugar, milk, egg yolks, and flour and cook until thickened, stirring frequently.
3. Add vanilla. Allow to cool.
4. Before serving, fold in whipped topping.

—*Barbie King, Spring Glen Farm Kitchens, Inc.*

◆

Cornstarch Pudding

Makes 6-8 serving

1 qt. milk
2 eggs, beaten
1 Tbsp. flour
1 Tbsp. cornstarch
3/4 cup sugar

1. Heat milk to scalding.
2. Combine beaten eggs, flour, cornstarch, and sugar. Add to milk.
3. Stir constantly until mixture thickens.
4. Cool. If desired, add whipped cream topping before serving.
—Mary Keeport Breighner, Rudy Breighner

Rice Pudding

Makes 6-8 servings

1/3 cup rice
1/3 cup granulated sugar
pinch of salt
1 1/2 Tbsp. butter
1 qt. milk

1. Mix all the ingredients in a greased 2- or 3-qt. baking dish.
2. Bake at 350° for about 2 1/2 hours, until rice is soft. Serve warm.
—Parke Plasterer, Pennsylvania Dutch Gifts

Butterscotch Apple Dessert

Makes 3 servings

1 Tbsp. butter
2 Tbsp. brown sugar
3 Tbsp. cream
2 cups apples, pared and sliced
whipped cream or whipped topping

1. Put butter, sugar, and cream in a saucepan and boil until ingredients are thickened.
2. Add apples and cook until soft.
3. Serve warm or cold with whipped cream or whipped topping.
—Helen A. Thomas, Thomas Produce

Apple Fritters
Makes 6-8 servings

1 cup flour
1½ tsp. baking powder
½ tsp. salt
2 Tbsp. sugar
1 egg, beaten
½ cup plus 1 Tbsp. milk
1½ cups apples, chopped

1. Mix first 6 ingredients together until smooth. Fold in chopped apples.
2. Heat a well-greased frying pan. Drop batter into frying pan to create mini-pancakes. Brown both sides.
3. Sprinkle with sugar and eat warm.

—Mrs. Sam Kauffman, Kauffman's Fruit Farms

Blueberry Dessert
Makes 20 servings

2 cups flour
½ lb. butter, softened
2 tsp. sugar

Filling:
8 oz. cream cheese
2 cups confectioners sugar
16-oz. container whipped topping

1 jar, or 2 21-oz. cans, blueberry pie filling

1. With a fork, mix together flour, butter, and 2 tsp. sugar. Press into an 11x14 baking pan.
2. Bake at 375° for 15 minutes. Cool.
3. Beat together cream cheese and sugar. Fold in whipped topping.
4. Spoon this mixture onto baked crust.
5. Spread blueberry pie filling on top.
6. Chill well before serving.

—Sallie Y. Lapp, Sunflower Foundation

◆

Petite Cherry Cheese Cakes

Makes 2 dozen

2 8-oz. pkgs. cream cheese, softened
3/4 cup sugar
2 eggs
1 Tbsp. lemon juice
1 tsp. vanilla
24 vanilla wafers
21-oz. can cherry pie filling

1. Beat cream cheese, sugar, eggs, lemon juice, and vanilla until light and fluffy.
2. Line small muffin pans with paper baking cups. Place one vanilla wafer in each cup.
3. Fill the cups 2/3 full with cream cheese mixture.
4. Bake for 15-20 minutes at 375° or until set.
5. Top each with about 1 Tbsp. cherry pie filling.
6. Chill and serve.

—Lorraine Good, Eisenberger's Bakery

Cherry Cheese Spread

Makes 12 servings

6-oz. pkg. cherry or strawberry gelatin
2 cups boiling water
1 medium-sized can crushed pineapple, drained
28-oz. can cherry or strawberry pie filling

Topping:
8 oz. cream cheese, softened
1 cup sour cream
1/4 cup granulated sugar

1/3 cup chopped nuts, to garnish (optional)

1. Mix together gelatin, water, pineapple, and pie filling. Spread into a 9x9 pan.
2. Combine topping ingredients. Spread topping over gelatin after gelatin is set.
3. Sprinkle with nuts, if desired.

—Ruth H. White, Chet's Flower Garden

◆

Peaches 'n Peach Sauce

Makes 8-10 servings

1 qt. peaches, peeled and diced
1 qt. water
3 oz. pkg. orange gelatin
1/2 cup sugar
1/4 cup clear jell

1. Cook peaches in 1 qt. water. Set aside.
2. Dissolve gelatin in 1 cup cold water. Stir in sugar.
3. Add clear jell to gelatin and sugar. Bring mixture to a boil. Chill.
4. Stir in peaches before serving as a light, refreshing dessert.
                              —*Edith Groff, Groff's Homegrown Produce*

Peach Cobbler

Makes 6-8 servings

3 cups peaches, sliced
3/4 cup baking mix
1/2 cup quick oats
1/2 cup brown sugar
1/2 tsp. cinnamon
2 Tbsp. butter, softened

1. Arrange peaches in a greased square baking dish.
2. Mix all dry ingredients together. Cut in butter until mixture is crumbly.
3. Sprinkle over peaches.
4. Bake at 375° for 30 minutes. Serve warm with milk or ice cream.
                              —*Ruth B. White, Brenneman Farms*

Rhubarb Dessert

Makes 8 servings

2 cups water
1/2 cup sugar
3 cups rhubarb, cut in 1/2-inch pieces
3-oz. pkg. red raspberry gelatin

1. Combine water and sugar. Bring to a boil.
2. Add rhubarb. Boil about 5 minutes, until rhubarb is soft.
3. Remove from heat. Add gelatin. Stir until gelatin dissolves.
4. Chill several hours before serving.
                              —*Katie Fisher, Shreiner's Flowers*

◆

Baked Rhubarb

Makes 6 servings

1 qt. rhubarb, cut in chunks
1 cup sugar
1-2 Tbsp. butter
dash of cinnamon

1. Mix rhubarb and sugar together.
2. Place rhubarb in a greased baking dish. Add butter and sprinkle cinnamon on top.
3. Cover dish.
4. Bake at 375° for 40-45 minutes.
5. Cool rhubarb. Serve with cream or over vanilla ice cream.

—*Elva E. Martin, Rudy Breighner*

Rhubarb Dream Dessert

Makes 12 servings

1 cup flour
5 Tbsp. powdered sugar
1/2 cup margarine, softened
2 eggs, beaten
1 1/2 cups sugar
1/4 cup flour
3/4 tsp. salt
3 cups rhubarb, chopped
1/2 tsp. nutmeg
1/2 cup raisins
1 Tbsp. margarine, melted
whipped cream (optional)

1. Combine flour, powdered sugar, and 1/2 cup margarine. Press into a 9x13 pan.
2. Bake for 15 minutes at 350°.
3. Mix together all remaining ingredients. Pour on top of crust.
4. Bake at 350° for 35 minutes.
5. Top with whipped cream when cooled, or serve with ice cream.

—*Mrs. Sam Kauffman, Kauffman's Fruit Farms*

◆

Frosty Strawberry Squares

Makes 10-12 servings

1 cup sifted flour
1/2 cup butter, melted
1/4 cup brown sugar, packed
1/2 cup nuts, chopped
2 egg whites, stiffly beaten
2 Tbsp. lemon juice
20 oz. frozen strawberries, partially thawed
2/3 cup sugar
8 oz. whipped topping

1. Mix together flour, butter, brown sugar, and nuts until crumbly. Spread evenly in a shallow pan.
2. Bake at 325° for 20 minutes, stirring occasionally. Cool.
3. Sprinkle 2/3 of crumbs in the bottom of a 9x13 dish.
4. Combine egg whites, lemon juice, berries, and sugar in a large bowl. Beat with an electric beater about 10 minutes, until stiff peaks form.
5. Fold in whipped topping.
6. Spoon over crumbs. Top with remaining crumbs.
7. Freeze for 6 hours or overnight. Cut in 10-12 squares.

Variation: 2 cups fresh strawberries may be used instead of frozen berries, but sugar should be increased from 2/3 cup to 1 cup.

—*Joyce G. Slaymaker, Slaymaker's Poultry*

Fruity Cubes

Makes 8-10 servings

3-oz. pkg. orange gelatin
3-oz. pkg. red gelatin
3-oz. pkg. lime gelatin
3 cups hot water
1 1/2 cups cold water
1 cup pineapple juice
1/4 cup sugar
3-oz. pkg. lemon gelatin
1/2 cup cold water
4 cups whipped topping

1. Prepare orange, red, and lime gelatin in three separate bowls, by adding 1 cup boiling water to each and stirring. When gelatin is dissolved, add 1/2 cup cold water to each bowl and stir.
2. Pour each gelatin into a different flat pan and chill until firm.

3. Heat pineapple juice and sugar together. Remove from heat.
4. Add lemon gelatin and 1/2 cup cold water. Chill until syrupy.
5. Add whipped topping to lemon mixture.
6. Cut orange, red, and green gelatins into small cubes.
7. Fold the gelatin cubes into the whipped topping mixture.
8. Chill about 6 hours before serving.

—Rachel King, Shreiner's Flowers

Frozen Fruit

4 cups sugar
2 qts. water
6 oz. can frozen orange juice concentrate
6 oz. can frozen lemonade concentrate
1 watermelon, cubed or balled
2 cantaloupes, cubed or balled
1 honeydew, cubed or balled
4 lbs. seedless grapes
4 lbs. peaches, sliced
1 1/2 lbs. blueberries

1. In a large saucepan, combine sugar and water. Bring to a boil. Stir in orange and lemonade concentrates. Cool.
2. In a large container, combine all fruits. Add cooled liquid.
3. Fill pint or quart freezer containers with fruit and freeze.

"This is an item you can do all at once at the end of the summer and have it handy throughout the year. It's refreshing and delicious. Serve it partially thawed; otherwise it gets mushy. I use it frequently as an appetizer for a company meal. Serve it alone or with a dab of sherbet on top."
—Joanne Warfel, S. Clyde Weaver, Inc.

Hot Fruit Sundaes
Makes 4 servings

8-oz. jar Shenk's "Nothing But" Fruit Spread, any flavor
1 pint fat free frozen yogurt

1. Heat open jar of Fruit Spread in microwave on high for 50 seconds.
2. Spoon 2 Tbsp. Fruit Spread over each serving of frozen yogurt.

This is a fat free dessert!
—Pat Zimmerman, Shenk's Cheese Co.

◆

Funnel Cakes

Makes 4-8 funnel cakes

2 eggs
1 cup milk
2 Tbsp. sugar
2 cups flour, sifted
1/4 tsp. salt
1 tsp. baking powder
oil
powdered sugar, to garnish

1. Beat eggs. Add milk and sugar.
2. Sift flour, salt, and baking powder together. Add dry ingredients to egg mixture. Mix together until smooth.
3. Heat oil in a frying pan at 375-400°.
4. Pour mixture into a funnel, while holding your finger over the bottom hole.
5. Let batter run through funnel and swirl into a design in the frying pan.
6. Fry until toasty brown. Remove from oil.
7. Place funnel cake on a plate and sprinkle with powdered sugar.
                    —Mary Kay McMichael, Givant's Jewish Baked Goods

Caramelized Popcorn

1 cup butter
3/8 cup light corn syrup
1 cup brown sugar
1/4 tsp. baking soda
1 tsp. vanilla
12 oz. Crispix cereal
1 bag popped microwave popcorn
2 cups peanuts or walnuts

1. Microwave butter, corn syrup, and brown sugar. Bring to a boil and stir.
2. Add baking soda and vanilla.
3. In a large bowl, mix cereal, popcorn, and nuts.
4. Pour liquid over cereal and bake for 1 hour at 225°, or microwave for 7 minutes, stirring halfway through.
                    —Joyce G. Slaymaker, Slaymaker's Poultry

◆

Cereal and Nut Treat
Makes 3¹/₂ qts.

1 stick butter
1¹/₂ cups brown sugar
1/4 cup light corn syrup
1/4 tsp. salt
1 tsp. cinnamon
3 cups Corn Chex
3 cups Rice Chex
3 cups Cheerios
1 cup nuts
1 cup raisins
1 cup pretzels, broken, optional
1 cup Cheez-Its, optional

1. In a saucepan heat butter, brown sugar, light corn syrup, salt, and cinnamon. Boil for 3 minutes.
2. Combine cereal, nuts, raisins, and additional ingredients.
3. Pour butter and brown sugar mixture over cereal. Mix gently.
4. Spread cereal on waxed-paper-covered cookie sheets to cool.
5. Break into chunks before serving or storing.

—Anne Wilson, Hodecker Celery Farm

Honey-Glazed Snack Mix
Makes 12 servings

1¹/₂ sticks butter
¹/₃ cup honey
³/₄ cup brown sugar
14 oz. Crispix cereal
1 cup mixed nuts or peanuts
1 cup mini-pretzels

1. Boil butter, honey, and sugar until thickened.
2. Combine cereal, nuts, and pretzels.
3. Pour honey mixture over cereal. Stir until well coated.
4. Place in a 9x13 pan.
5. Bake at 275° for 45 minutes, stirring several times.
6. Remove from oven. Spread on waxed paper to cool.
7. Break into chunks before servings or storing.

—Elva E. Martin, Rudy Breighner

Mocha Truffles

Makes 5 1/2 dozen truffles

24 oz. semi-sweet chocolate chips
8 oz. cream cheese, softened
3 Tbsp. instant coffee granules
2 tsp. water
1 lb. dark confectionary coating
white confectionary coating, optional

1. Melt chocolate chips in a double boiler. Add cream cheese, coffee granules, and water. Mix well.
2. Chill until firm enough to shape.
3. Shape into 1-inch balls and place on cookie sheets lined with waxed paper.
4. Chill 1-2 hours or until firm.
5. Slowly melt chocolate coating in double boiler.
6. Dip balls into chocolate. Place on waxed paper to harden.
7. If desired, melt white coating and drizzle over truffles.

—Joanne Warfel, S. Clyde Weaver, Inc.

Butter Toffee Candy

1 cup sugar
1/2 tsp. salt
1/4 cup water
1/2 cup butter
3/4 cup walnuts
12 oz. semi-sweet chocolate morsels

1. Mix sugar, salt, water, and butter in medium saucepan. Cook over medium heat, stirring occasionally, until mixture comes to a boil.
2. After it begins to boil, do not stir. Continue to cook until it reaches the light crack stage (285° on candy thermometer).
3. Add 1/2 cup nuts. Pour onto greased cookie sheet. Spread thin with buttered fingers or a spoon. Cool.
4. Melt semi-sweet morsels. Spread on top of candy. Sprinkle with remaining 1/4 cup nuts.
5. Once chocolate has hardened, break candy into bite-sized pieces. Store in a candy tin.

"Christmas Day just doesn't seem complete until you have some of Grandma Breneman's Butter Toffee. Her three grown boys still wait for her to bring out the candy. She serves it after dinner while Uncle Roy tells one of his many stories about growing up on the farm."

—Kathy Funk, Viv's Varieties

◆

Pecan Delights

Makes 4 dozen

2¼ cups packed brown sugar
1 cup butter or margarine
1 cup light corn syrup
⅛ tsp. salt
14 oz. sweetened condensed milk
1 tsp. vanilla extract
1½ lbs. whole pecans
6 oz. semi-sweet chocolate chips
6 oz. milk chocolate chips
2 Tbsp. shortening

1. In a large saucepan, combine sugar, butter or margarine, corn syrup, and salt. Cook over medium heat until all sugar is dissolved.
2. Gradually add milk. Mix well.
3. Continue cooking until candy thermometer reads 248° (firm ball stage).
4. Remove from heat. Stir in vanilla. Fold in pecans.
5. When cooled slightly, drop by teaspoonsful onto a waxed-paper-lined cookie sheet. Chill until firm.
6. Melt chocolate chips and shortening in microwave or double boiler. Drizzle chocolate over each cluster.

"These candies have become a holiday favorite to both make and eat. This is one of the delicious kinds of candy that a couple of us from work got together to make at Easter time. It was fun getting together, plus we had some delicious treats to share with our families and friends."
—*Arlene Leaman, S. Clyde Weaver, Inc.*

Peanut Butter Crispy Eggs

Makes 5-6 dozen eggs

½ cup butter, softened
1 lb. confectioners sugar
28 oz. peanut butter
5½ cups crispy rice cereal
1 lb. chocolate

1. Mix butter and confectioners sugar together.
2. Add peanut butter and blend well.
3. Add cereal. Mixture may be blended with hands, if necessary.
4. Form small eggs out of the mixture. Place eggs on cookie sheets lined with waxed paper. Refrigerate eggs until cold and firm.
5. Melt chocolate and dip eggs into it.
—*Barbara Finefrock, Willow Valley Farm*

◆

Peanut Butter Candy
Makes 6 dozen

4 oz. cream cheese, softened
4 Tbsp. margarine, softened
1 Tbsp. milk or water
1½ lbs. (approx.) confectioners sugar
1 cup peanut butter
1 tsp. vanilla
1 lb. coating chocolate

1. Mix together all ingredients, except coating chocolate.
2. Roll this mixture into balls about 1-inch in diameter. Refrigerate.
3. Slowly melt coating chocolate in double boiler.
4. Dip balls into chocolate. Place on waxed paper to harden.

"My family thinks these are a must at Christmas."
                    —*Dorothy Nolt, Chet's Flower Garden*

Creamy Caramels
Makes 64 pieces

1 cup sugar
1 cup dark corn syrup
1 cup butter or margarine
14-oz. can sweetened condensed milk
1 tsp. vanilla extract

1. Line an 8x8 pan with buttered foil. Set aside.
2. Combine sugar, corn syrup, and butter in a 3-qt. saucepan. Bring to a boil over medium heat, stirring constantly. Boil slowly for 4 minutes, without stirring.
3. Remove from heat and stir in milk.
4. Reduce heat to medium-low and cook until candy thermometer reads 232° (soft ball stage), stirring constantly.
5. Remove from heat. Sir in vanilla.
6. Pour into greased pan. Cool.
7. Remove from pan and cut into 1" squares.
8. Wrap each piece individually in waxed paper and twist ends.
                    —*Arlene Leaman, S. Clyde Weaver, Inc.*

◆

Maple Taffy

1/2 cup sugar
3/4 cup light corn syrup
3/4 cup maple syrup
1/3 cup water
1 1/2 Tbsp. butter
1/8 tsp. soda, without lumps

1. Place sugar, corn syrup, maple syrup, and water into a saucepan. Cook slowly, stirring constantly until sugar is dissolved. Continue cooking until mixture reaches 275° (slightly brittle when dropped in cold water).
2. Remove from heat. Add butter and soda, stirring just enough to mix well. If stirred too much, the taffy will sugar.
3. Pour into a greased pan. Let stand until taffy is cool enough to handle.
4. Gather into a ball and pull until light in color and quite firm.
5. Stretch out into a long rope and cut into pieces with a scissors.
6. Wrap each piece in waxed paper.

—Elton Moshier, Pure Maple Syrup

Maple Sugar Candy

maple syrup

1. Boil maple syrup in a saucepan or kettle to 238°. Cool slightly.
2. Stir constantly until syrup begins to look creamy and loses its gloss.
3. Pour immediately into greased rubber molds or cookie tins. Allow to harden. Cut candy on cookie tins into squares.

—Elton Moshier, Pure Maple Syrup

Maple Cream

maple syrup

1. Boil maple syrup to 224°. Cool to room temperature (1-1 1/2 hours).
2. Beat. Cool. Beat again on slow speed.
3. Store in an airtight container. Stir before serving.
4. Spread on bread, toast, or crackers.

—Elton Moshier, Pure Maple Syrup

◆

Maple Wax

2 or more cups of maple syrup

1. Cook maple syrup in a saucepan until it reaches 246° (forms a firm ball when dropped in cold water).
2. Pour hot syrup in a thin stream over snow or ice. As syrup touches the snow it will harden and form a wax-like rope.
3. Prepare a plate of snow for each person, or a large dish for a number of people to use. Eat the maple wax directly from the snow using a fork.

—Elton Moshier, Pure Maple Syrup

Maple Ice Cream

4 eggs
1/2 cup sugar
1 cup maple syrup
1 cup milk
1 cup heavy cream
1 cup almonds, blanched, browned, and chopped, optional

1. Beat eggs until very light. Add sugar and maple syrup and beat again.
2. Scald milk. Add it slowly to the egg mixture, stirring constantly.
3. Cook mixture in a double boiler until it coats the spoon, stirring constantly.
4. Remove from heat and beat with egg beater until light.
5. Cool. Add cream. Freeze, using three parts crushed ice to one part salt.
6. Sprinkle almonds over ice cream before serving.

—Elton Moshier, Pure Maple Syrup

The first time I came to Central Market was in 1943 when my friend's father, Jacob Carper, needed help at his stand because he had to attend a funeral. My biggest fear was not knowing how to read the scales to figure out the price of the freshly dressed chickens. So he priced them all before he left! I made friends and talked with the neighboring standholders—Mrs. Avory Hess, Mrs. Shertzer, and Great-Grandpa Stoner.

The next week Mrs. Ruth Brubaker called and offered me a job at Market. I sold home-grown celery, red beets, rhubarb, onions, eggs, and bunched carrots for her. Frank Enck's Deli was the next stand I worked on, and in 1961 I started bringing our own carnations to our present stand.

—Anna Marie Groff, Anna Marie Groff's Fresh Cut Flowers

Cinnamon Apple Cake with Almond Cream Cheese Frosting

Makes 8 servings

Cake:
1¹/2 cups flour
¹/2 tsp. salt
1¹/2 tsp. baking soda
2 tsp. cinnamon
¹/2 cup white sugar
¹/2 cup butter or margarine, softened
2 eggs
¹/2 tsp. vanilla
4 cups apples, coarsely chopped
³/4 cup walnuts, chopped

Frosting:
¹/4 cup butter, softened
4 oz. cream cheese, softened
¹/8 tsp. almond extract
confectioner sugar—up to 8 oz., or enough to make a
    good spreading consistency

1. Preheat oven to 325°.
2. Butter and flour an 8" round cake pan. Line bottom of pan with waxed paper. Butter and dust waxed paper with flour.
3. Combine flour, salt, baking soda, and cinnamon. Set aside.
4. Cream sugar and butter with an electric beater until light and fluffy. Add eggs and vanilla. Beat well.
5. Gradually add flour mixture. Continue beating until combined. Fold in apples and walnuts until just blended.
6. Spread batter into cake pan.
7. Bake at 325° for 50-55 minutes until toothpick inserted in center comes out clean.
8. Allow to cool for 10 minutes. Invert cake on a wire rack to cool. Remove waxed paper.
9. Cream butter, cream cheese, and almond extract for frosting.
10. Gradually blend in sugar until the desired consistency is reached. (We keep it fairly light and creamy.)
11. Spread frosting over top and sides of cake. Cover and refrigerate overnight.

"I adapted this recipe from one created for dieters. I removed the fruit juice and imitation ingredients and did exactly what my grandmother said was the secret of good baking . . . I DOUBLED the quantities of the 'good ingredients.' This tasty cake is not for calorie counters!"
                            —Andy Shaw, customer of John R. Stoner Produce

♦

Caramel Apple Cake

Makes 12-16 servings

Cake:
1¹/₂ cups vegetable oil
1¹/₂ cups sugar
¹/₂ cup packed brown sugar
3 eggs
2 cups flour
2 tsp. ground cinnamon
¹/₂ tsp. ground nutmeg
1 tsp. baking soda
¹/₂ tsp. salt
3¹/₂ cups apples, peeled and diced
1 cup walnuts, chopped
2 tsp. vanilla

Icing:
¹/₂ cup brown sugar, packed
¹/₃ cup light cream
¹/₄ cup butter or margarine
dash of salt
1 cup confectioners sugar
chopped walnuts (optional)

1. In a large mixing bowl, combine oil and sugars. Add eggs one at a time, beating well after each addition.
2. In a separate bowl, combine flour, cinnamon, nutmeg, soda, and salt. Add dry ingredients to creamed mixture. Beat well.
3. Fold in apples, walnuts, and vanilla.
4. Pour batter into a greased and floured 10" tube pan.
5. Bake at 325° for 1¹/₂ hours, or until cake is done.
6. Cool cake in pan for 10 minutes; then place cake on a wire rack to cool completely.
7. In top of a double boiler over simmering water, heat brown sugar, cream, butter, and salt until sugar is dissolved. Cool at room temperature.
8. Beat in confectioners sugar until smooth.
9. Drizzle icing over cake. Sprinkle with walnuts if desired.

—*Viv Hunt, Viv's Varieties*

The Arcade Market began in 1927 in the block between Orange and Marion Streets and Prince and Market Streets. The farmers market continued until 1965; the entire building was demolished in 1969. The Prince Street parking garage now occupies the site.

◆

Blueberry Cake
with Streusel Topping
Makes 9-12 servings

Streusel:
1/4 cup sugar
1/4 cup brown sugar
1/3 cup flour
1/2 tsp. cinnamon
1/4 cup butter or margarine, softened

Cake:
6 Tbsp. butter or margarine, softened
3/4 cup sugar
1 egg
2 cups flour
3 Tbsp. cornstarch
2 tsp. baking powder
1/4 tsp. salt
1 tsp. vanilla
1/2 cup milk
2 cups blueberries

1. Mix together dry streusel ingredients. Cut in butter or margarine until mixture is crumbly. Set aside.
2. In a large bowl, cream together butter, sugar, and egg. Add flour, cornstarch, baking powder, salt, vanilla, and milk. Mix well.
3. Fold in blueberries.
4. Pour batter into a greased 9x9 pan.
5. Sprinkle streusel on top.
6. Bake at 375° for 40-45 minutes.

—*Barbie King, Spring Glen Farm Kitchens, Inc.*

In the 1920s, a market boy charged from 10¢ to 25¢ for transporting a customer's market basket, depending on the length of the trip. For carrying a basket around as a person shopped, a youngster was paid 10¢. A boy might make as many as a dozen trips in a day. The distance could range from a short walk to the trolley or bus stop, to going more than a mile. A few boys specialized in long-distance traveling and equipped their bicycles to carry baskets. Some shoppers did not accompany the delivery boy home but arranged to have their market baskets deposited on back-door steps while they did additional shopping. Boys could also earn extra money helping standholders to unload and load their wares.

◆

Cherry Streusel Cake

Makes 15 servings

1¹/2 cups flour
1 cup sugar
3 tsp. baking powder
2 eggs
³/4 cup milk
5 Tbsp. butter or margarine, melted
1 tsp. vanilla
1 qt. sour cherries, drained

Crumb Topping:
1¹/2 cups flour
1¹/4 cups sugar
1 rounded tsp. cinnamon
³/4-1 cup butter or margarine, softened

1. Sift together 1¹/2 cups flour, 1 cup sugar, and baking powder.
2. Put eggs in a small bowl. Add milk. Beat eggs and milk together.
3. Combine eggs and milk with flour mixture.
4. Add melted butter and vanilla. Beat well.
5. Pour batter into greased and floured 9x13 pan. Spread cherries over batter.
6. Combine all dry crumb topping ingredients. Cut butter into crumbs until mixture becomes crumbly.
7. Cover cake with crumb topping.
8. Bake for 10 minutes at 400°.
9. Reduce heat to 375° and bake for 30 minutes.

"This is a favorite served right from the oven. Put a piece of warm cake in a bowl and cover it with milk. Of course, some 'English' folks prefer it cold!"
—Mary Kay McMichael, Givant's Jewish Baked Goods

Cherry Cream Torte

Makes 16-18 servings

6 oz. ladyfingers
2 Tbsp. white grape juice or apple juice
8 oz. cream cheese, softened
²/3 cup sugar
1 tsp. almond extract, divided
2 cups whipping cream, whipped
21 oz. can cherry pie filling
toasted sliced almonds, to garnish, optional
whipped cream, to garnish, optional

1. Split ladyfingers lengthwise. Brush with juice.
2. Place a layer of ladyfingers around the sides and bottom of a lightly greased 9" springform pan.
3. In a mixing bowl, beat cream cheese until smooth. Add sugar and 1/2 tsp. almond extract. Beat on medium speed for 1 minute.
4. Fold in whipped cream. Spread half of mixture over crust.
5. Arrange remaining ladyfingers in a spoke-like fashion on top of cream cheese mixture. Spread evenly with remaining cream cheese mixture.
6. Cover and chill overnight.
7. Combine pie filling and remaining extract. Spread over cream cheese layer.
8. Chill at least 2 hours. To serve, remove sides of pan.
9. Garnish with almonds and whipped cream, if desired.

—Joyce G. Slaymaker, Slaymaker's Poultry

Plum Cake

Makes 12-15 servings

2 cups flour
1 3/4 cups sugar
1/2 tsp. salt
1/2 tsp. baking powder
1/2 tsp. baking soda
1 tsp. cinnamon
1/2 tsp. ground cloves
3/4 cup vegetable oil
3 eggs
2 4 3/4-oz. jars strained plums
1 cup pecans, chopped

Lemon Glaze:
2/3 cup confectioners sugar
2 tsp. water
1 1/2 tsp. lemon juice

1. Beat together all cake ingredients except pecans. Blend until thoroughly combined. Stir in pecans.
2. Using vegetable shortening, grease a 10" tube pan or bundt pan. Flour pan. Pour batter into pan.
3. Bake at 300° for 1 hour and 15 minutes. Cool slightly and then remove from pan.
4. Combine all glaze ingredients.
6. Spoon glaze over top of warm cake, allowing it to drizzle down the sides.
7. Cool thoroughly before serving.

—Dorothy Nolt, Chet's Flower Garden

◆────────

Quick Pineapple Dessert
Makes 12-15 servings

1 cup flour
1 cup brown sugar
1 tsp. baking soda
1/8 tsp. salt
1 egg
8 1/2-oz. can crushed pineapple and juice

Topping:
1/4 cup brown sugar
1/4 cup chopped nuts

1. Place all cake ingredients in a bowl and mix thoroughly.
2. Pour batter into a greased 8x12 pan. Sprinkle topping over cake.
3. Bake at 350° for 30-40 minutes.
4. Serve with milk, ice cream, or whipped cream.
—*Sara Jane Wenger, Chet's Flower Garden*

The New Era, Lancaster, Saturday, October 5, 1889

The Central Market, A City Edifice to be Proud Of
A fine example of the Romanesque Style of Architecture
which Reflects Credit on the Architect and Contractor.
Good Accommodations

The near completion of the new Central Market House, built by the City of Lancaster to take the place of the unsightly old structures that formerly stood in the rear of the City Hall, has induced us to publish today's full description of the beautiful new structure . . .

Of the several plans presented, that of Mr. James H. Warner, formerly of London, England, but now a resident of our city, was the one adopted at the meeting of City Council held March 23. He was also engaged to superintend the building operations and the result is the possession by Lancaster of one of the finest market houses in the State . . . Rains have interfered greatly with the work and prevented it being carried forward as rapidly as it would have been had the weather been more favorable, but, nevertheless, the contractors have nearly completed the building at the specified time and the work has been well done. Material and workmanship have been of the best and the structure is one that will last many years. It is a market house of which our people may well feel proud, for it combines to a marked degree the properties of architectural beauty, durability, comfort, and convenience, besides being so arranged as to secure the best sanitary conditions.

Pumpkin Cake

Makes 15 servings

2 cups sugar
2 cups flour
4 eggs
2 tsp. baking powder
2 tsp. cinnamon
2 cups pumpkin, mashed
1 cup vegetable oil
2 tsp. baking soda
1/2 tsp. salt
1/2 cup coconut
1/2 cup English walnuts

Frosting:
1/4 cup butter or margarine, softened
2 cups confectioners sugar
3 oz. cream cheese, softened
1 tsp. vanilla

1. Stir all cake ingredients together, except the coconut and walnuts, and blend well with a mixer.
2. Fold in coconut and walnuts by hand.
3. Pour batter into a greased 9x13 pan.
4. Bake at 350° for 35 minutes.
5. Cream together frosting ingredients. Spread frosting on cooled cake.

—*Kitty Longenecker, Givant's Jewish Baked Goods*

◆

Pumpkin Torte
Makes 15 servings

Crust:
1³/4 cups graham cracker crumbs
1/3 cup brown sugar
1/2 cup butter, melted

Filling #1:
3 eggs
3/4 cup sugar
8 oz. cream cheese, softened

Filling #2:
1 env. unflavored gelatin
1/4 cup cold water
2 cups pumpkin
1/2 cup sugar
1/2 cup milk
1/2 tsp. salt
1 tsp. cinnamon
3 egg whites

whipped topping, to garnish

1. Mix crust ingredients together. Press crust mixture into bottom of a greased 9x13 cake pan.
2. Beat ingredients for Filling #1 together. Pour filling over crust.
3. Bake at 350° for 10-20 minutes.
4. Soak gelatin in water.
5. Cook pumpkin, sugar, milk, salt, and cinnamon together until mixture bubbles. Add gelatin mixture to cooked pumpkin mixture. Stir. Cool.
6. Beat egg whites until stiff. Fold into cooled pumpkin mixture.
7. Pour Filling #2 into pan, on top of Filling #1. Allow to cool thoroughly.
8. Top with whipped topping before serving.

—Lois Thomas, C.H. Thomas Meats

Cooking Tip

Add chopped herbs, such as thyme or dill, to water and pour into an ice cube tray. Freeze. Then place one or two cubes in a soup or sauce as needed.

—Ethel Stoner, John R. Stoner Produce

Rhubarb Coffee Cake

Makes 15 servings

Cake:
1/2 cup butter or margarine, softened
1/2 cup brown sugar, packed
1/4 cup sugar
1 egg
1 tsp. vanilla
11/4 cups flour
3/4 cup whole wheat flour
1 tsp. baking powder
1/2 tsp. baking soda
1/4 tsp. salt
1/4 tsp. cinnamon
1 cup buttermilk
2 cups rhubarb, diced—fresh or frozen

Topping:
1/4 cup brown sugar
11/2 tsp. ground cinnamon
1/2 cup walnuts, chopped

1. In a mixing bowl, cream butter and sugars together. Add egg and vanilla. Beat until fluffy.
2. In a separate bowl, combine flours, baking powder, baking soda, salt, and cinnamon.
3. Add dry mixture to creamed ingredients alternately with buttermilk, mixing well after each addition.
4. Stir in rhubarb.
5. Pour into a greased 9x13 baking pan.
6. Combine topping ingredients and sprinkle evenly over batter.
7. Bake at 350° for 35 minutes.
8. Serve warm or at room temperature.

"My mother who is 88 grows wonderful strawberry rhubarb!"
　　　　　　　　　　　　　　　　　—Viv Hunt, Viv's Varieties

◆

Strawberry-Rhubarb Coffee Cake

Makes 15 servings

Filling:
3 cups rhubarb, sliced—fresh or frozen
1 qt. fresh strawberries, mashed
2 Tbsp. lemon juice
1/3 cup cornstarch
1 cup sugar

Cake:
3 cups flour
1 cup sugar
1 tsp. baking powder
1 tsp. baking soda
1/2 tsp. salt
1 cup butter or margarine, softened
1 1/2 cups buttermilk
2 eggs
1 tsp. vanilla

Topping:
1/4 cup butter or margarine
3/4 cup flour
3/4 cup sugar

1. In a large saucepan, combine rhubarb, strawberries, and lemon juice. Cover and cook over medium heat for 5 minutes.
2. Combine cornstarch and sugar. Stir into saucepan.
3. Bring mixture to a boil, stirring constantly until thickened. Remove from heat and set aside.
4. In a large bowl, combine flour, sugar, baking powder, baking soda, and salt.
5. Cut in butter until mixture resembles coarse crumbs.
6. Beat buttermilk, eggs, and vanilla together. Stir into crumb mixture.
7. Spread about half of batter into a greased 9x13 baking dish. Carefully spread fruit filling on top. Drop remaining batter by tablespoonsful over filling.
8. For topping, melt butter in a saucepan over low heat.
9. Remove from heat and stir in flour and sugar until mixture resembles coarse crumbs. Sprinkle over batter.
10. Lay foil on lower oven rack to catch any juicy fruit spills.
11. Bake at 350° for 40-50 minutes or longer. Cool in pan. Cut in squares.
—*Joanne Warfel, S. Clyde Weaver, Inc.*

Strawberry Angel Dessert

Makes 12-16 servings

2 cups fresh strawberries
1/3 cup sugar
3-oz. pkg. strawberry-flavored gelatin
1 cup boiling water
4 cups (12 oz.) whipped topping
10" angel food cake, baked

1. Crush berries slightly. Add sugar. Let berries sit for 5 minutes. Drain berries, reserving syrup.
2. Dissolve gelatin in boiling water. Add reserved syrup.
3. Chill gelatin just until it begins to congeal. Beat it lightly until fluffy.
4. Fold in whipped topping.
5. Chill mixture until it reaches a spreading consistency. Fold in berries.
6. Slice cake horizontally into 3 layers. Spread the berry mixture between the layers. Sides may be iced, if desired.
7. Chill until serving time.

—*Arlene Leaman, S. Clyde Weaver, Inc.*

Coconut Cake

Makes 3 8" round cake layers

1 cup shortening
1 3/4 cups sugar
4 eggs, separated
3 1/4 cups cake flour
1/2 tsp. salt
2 1/2 tsp. baking powder
1 cup milk
1 tsp. vanilla
1 cup coconut, grated

1. Cream shortening. Add sugar gradually. Beat until fluffy.
2. Add egg yolks and beat them in.
3. Sift all dry ingredients together twice.
4. Add dry ingredients to creamed mixture, alternating with milk and vanilla. Beat thoroughly after each addition.
5. Beat egg whites in separate bowl until stiff.
6. Fold coconut and stiffly beaten egg whites into batter.
7. Pour into 3 greased and floured layer pans.
8. Bake at 350° for 30 minutes. Cool. Spread icing between 3 cake layers and over sides and top before serving.

—*Dorothy W. Stauffer, Nye's Sandwich Haus*

◆

Buttermilk Spice Cake

Makes 15 servings

2¹/2 cups flour
1 cup sugar
³/4 cup brown sugar
1 tsp. baking powder
1 tsp. baking soda
1 tsp. salt
³/4 tsp. cinnamon
³/4 tsp. allspice
¹/2 tsp. cloves
¹/2 tsp. nutmeg
1¹/3 cups buttermilk
¹/2 cup shortening
3 eggs

1. Heat oven to 350°. Grease and flour a 9x13 baking pan.
2. Measure all cake ingredients into a large mixer bowl.
3. Blend for 30 seconds on low speed, scraping bowl constantly.
4. Beat for 3 minutes on high speed, scraping bowl occasionally.
5. Pour batter into cake pan.
6. Bake for 45 minutes, or until toothpick inserted in center comes out clean.
7. Cool.
8. Spread with Butterscotch Broiled Topping.

Butterscotch Broiled Topping

¹/4 cup butter or margarine, softened
²/3 cup brown sugar, packed
1 cup nuts, finely chopped
2 Tbsp. milk

1. Mix butter, brown sugar, and nuts thoroughly. Stir in milk.
2. Spread mixture evenly over warm 9x13 cake.
3. Set oven to broil.
4. Place cake 5" from heat. Broil about 3 minutes, or until topping bubbles and browns slightly. Watch carefully. Topping burns easily!

—*Ann F. Kreider, Viv's Varieties*

Fruit Cake

Makes 15-20 servings

1 lb. light brown sugar
1/2 lb. butter, at room temperature
3 eggs, beaten
1 tsp. soda
3 cups flour
1 tsp. ground cloves
1 cup sweet milk
1 lb. raisins
1/2 lb. dates
1/2 lb. currants
1/2 lb. citron
1/4 lb. candied lemon
1/4 lb. candied orange
1 lb. nuts
1/2 cup fruit juice
1 tsp. vanilla

1. Cream sugar and butter.
2. Add beaten eggs.
3. Sift together soda, flour, and cloves.
4. Add milk alternately with dry ingredients to creamed mixture. Set this batter aside.
5. In a separate bowl, combine all other ingredients, except fruit juice and vanilla.
6. Pour batter, fruit juice, and vanilla over fruit and nut mixture. Fold together gently.
7. Line a tube cake pan with waxed paper. Pour in mixed cake batter.
8. Bake for 3 hours at 300°.

"My mother always baked a fruit cake to treat guests. She baked it weeks before Christmas and kept it in a can."

—Helen A. Thomas, Thomas Produce

The North American, Philadelphia, Sunday, July 5, 1908

How Is This for a Housewife's Paradise?

Mayor J.P. McCaskey naturally regards Lancaster with pride.
"There is no doubt the markets are about the finest and cheapest in the country," he declared. "The people of the country get their wealth from the soil—they don't depend upon Wall Street."

◆

Short Cake
Makes 6-8 servings

Cake:
2 cups flour
3 tsp. baking powder
3/4 tsp. salt
2 Tbsp. sugar
1/3 cup shortening
2/3 cup milk
1 egg, beaten

Topping:
1/2 cup sugar
1/2 cup flour
3 Tbsp. butter, softened

1. Combine flour, baking powder, salt, and sugar. Cut in shortening until mixture forms small crumbs.
2. Add milk and egg. Mix well. Pour batter into greased round cake pan.
3. Combine dry topping ingredients. Cut in butter until mixture becomes crumbly.
4. Crumble the topping ingredients on top of the cake batter.
5. Bake at 350° until toothpick inserted in the middle comes out clean.
6. Serve with fresh fruit and milk.

—Annie Jean Miller, Sunflower Floudation

Punch Bowl Cake
Makes 15 servings

2 layers yellow cake
21-oz. can cherry pie filling
15-oz. can crushed pineapple
5.1-oz. box instant vanilla pudding, prepared
15-oz. can fruit cocktail
1/2-1 cup coconut, grated
1 cup nuts, chopped
16-oz. container whipped topping

1. Prepare your favorite yellow cake. Cut cake into 1" cubes.
2. Line bottom and sides of a large serving bowl or punch bowl with cake cubes.
3. Layer remaining ingredients in the bowl, in the order they are listed.
4. Chill well overnight before serving.

—Joyce G. Slaymaker, Slaymaker's Poultry

Peanut Butter Tandy Kakes

Makes 36 small pieces

4 eggs
2 cups sugar
1 tsp. vanilla
1 tsp. oil
2 cups flour
dash of salt
2 tsp. baking powder
1 cup milk
1 cup peanut butter
8 oz. chocolate candy bar
1 Tbsp. oil

1. Beat together eggs, sugar, vanilla, and 1 tsp. oil.
2. Add flour, salt, baking powder, and milk. Mix well.
3. Lightly grease an 11x16 cookie sheet with 1" sides. Spread batter into pan.
4. Bake at 350° for 25 minutes.
5. As soon as cake is removed from oven, spread peanut butter over top.
6. Refrigerate cake until peanut butter is firm.
7. When cake is cool, melt chocolate with 1 Tbsp. oil. Spread chocolate over the cake. Refrigerate.
8. When chocolate is cooled, cake is ready to serve.

—Barbara Finefrock, Willow Valley Farm

Fun with Sponge Cake

Makes 1 serving

1 piece sponge cake, cut any size
whipped topping
2 apricot halves

1. Spread whipped topping on cake.
2. Top with 2 apricot halves, so it looks like 2 eggs on toast.

—Helen A. Thomas, Thomas Produce

The Eastern Market was a farmers market located on the southeast corner of King and Shippen Streets. It had about 200 stalls. The unique Second-Empire-style architecture featured towers which could be viewed over a large part of the city. The market closed in 1918. The building has been renovated and is now used for offices.

COOKIES

Nana's Molasses Cookies
Makes 24-30 cookies

3/4 cup shortening or butter
1 cup sugar
1/4 cup molasses
1 egg
2 cups flour, sifted
2 tsp. baking soda
1/2 tsp. cloves
1/2 tsp. ginger
1 tsp. cinnamon
1/2 tsp. salt
colored sugar

1. Melt shortening. Allow to cool.
2. Add sugar, molasses, and egg. Beat well.
3. Sift together flour, soda, cloves, ginger, cinnamon, and salt.
4. Add to batter. Blend well.
5. Chill for several hours or overnight.
6. Form into walnut-sized balls. Dip into colored sugar and place on ungreased cookie sheet.
7. Bake for 8-10 minutes at 375°. Do not overbake. Allow to cool.

"This recipe is from my grandmother, who loved to bake and baked these cookies until she was in her early 90s! They were traditionally a Christmas cookie in our home. Very flavorful, great for dunking in milk."
—Gail Johnson, customer of Viv's Varieties, Sensenig's, and others

Market boys had their greatest opportunity to earn money carrying shoppers' baskets on Saturday mornings and during evening market hours. Some of the more energetic youth managed to get in a few trips early in the mornings and during lunch breaks throughout the school year. Truant officers kept a special lookout for industrious hooky-players at the market houses. A speedy youth could earn a decent day's wages, but he needed to be steady and agile. Being in too much of a hurry often meant an upset wagon, with apples, oranges, and potatoes rolling down the street.

◆

Banana Fudge-Walnut Brownies
Makes 16 brownies

1/4 cup margarine
6 oz. semi-sweet chocolate chips
3/4 cup flour
1/2 cup sugar
1/3 cup walnuts, chopped
1/3 cup ripe banana, mashed
1/2 tsp. vanilla
1/4 tsp. baking powder
1/4 tsp. salt
1 egg

1. In a 2-qt. saucepan over low heat, melt margarine or butter and choco-late chips, stirring constantly. Add remaining ingredients.
2. Grease the bottom of an 8x8 pan. Spread batter into pan.
3. Bake at 350° for 30 minutes or until center is set.
4. Cool completely. Cut into 2" squares.

—Joyce G. Slaymaker, Slaymaker's Poultry

Black-Bottom Banana Bars
Makes 36 squares

1/4 cup butter or margarine, softened
1 cup sugar
1 egg
1 tsp. vanilla
1 1/2 cups ripe bananas, mashed
1 1/2 cups flour
1 tsp. baking powder
1 tsp. baking soda
1/2 tsp. salt
1/4 cup baking cocoa

1. In a mixing bowl cream together butter and sugar. Add egg and vanilla. Beat until thoroughly combined. Blend in bananas.
2. In a separate bowl, combine flour, baking powder, baking soda, and salt. Add to creamed mixture and blend well. Divide batter in half.
3. Add cocoa to half of batter. Spread this into a greased 9x13 baking pan.
4. Spoon remaining batter on top and swirl it with a knife.
5. Bake at 350° for 25 minutes or until the bars are done. Cool.

"This is a delicious way to use over-ripe bananas. These bars are even bet-ter the second day, and they stay very moist!"

—Joyce G. Slaymaker, Slaymaker's Poultry

◆

Butter Tart Pan Squares

Makes 16 squares

1/2 cup margarine, softened
1 cup flour, sifted
2 Tbsp. sugar
2 eggs, beaten
1 1/2 cups brown sugar
3 Tbsp. flour
1/2 tsp. baking powder
1 tsp. vanilla
1/2 cup walnuts, chopped

1. Cream margarine. Mix in 1 cup flour and 2 Tbsp. sugar.
2. Press into an ungreased 9x9 pan.
3. Bake at 350° for 15 minutes.
4. Mix remaining ingredients together. Pour and spread over baked layer.
5. Return pan to oven. Bake 20-30 more minutes.
5. Cool before cutting.

—Joyce G. Slaymaker, Slaymaker's Poultry

Chocolate Chip Cookies

Makes 3 dozen cookies

1 cup brown sugar
1/2 cup granulated sugar
1 cup shortening
2 eggs
1/2 tsp. vanilla
2 1/4 cups flour
1 tsp. salt
1/2 tsp. baking soda
1 1/2 cups chocolate chips

1. Cream together sugars and shortening.
2. Stir in other ingredients, adding chocolate chips last.
3. Drop by teaspoonsful onto ungreased cookie sheet.
4. Bake at 350° for 8-10 minutes.

—Marian King, Shreiner's Flowers

Chocolate Mint Squares

Makes 24-36 squares

1 cup sugar
1/2 cup margarine, softened
4 eggs
1 cup flour
1/2 tsp. salt
1 tsp. vanilla
16-oz. can chocolate syrup

Topping:
2 cups confectioners sugar
2 Tbsp. creme de menthe
1/2 cup butter or margarine, softened
6 oz. chocolate chips
6 Tbsp. margarine, melted

1. Cream together sugar, 1/2 cup margarine, and eggs.
2. Stir in flour, salt, vanilla, and chocolate syrup.
3. Pour into a greased 9x13 pan.
4. Bake for 30 minutes at 350°. Cool.
5. To make the topping, mix together sugar, creme de menthe and 1/2 cup butter or margarine. Cool.
6. Spread mint layer over cooled batter.
7. Melt together chocolate chips and 6 Tbsp. margarine. Drizzle over mint layer. Refrigerate. Cut into squares when chocolate is firm, but before it hardens.

—Annie Jean Miller, Sunflower Foundation

Crispy Bars

Makes 24-30 bars

1 cup corn syrup
1 cup sugar
1 cup peanut butter
6 cups crispy rice cereal
12 oz. chocolate chips

1. Melt corn syrup and sugar just until boiling. Remove from heat.
2. Stir in peanut butter until melted. Add cereal. Mix well.
3. Spread into a greased 9x13 pan.
4. Melt chocolate chips. Spread chocolate over cereal.
5. Cool. Cut into bars and serve.

—Lena King, John R. Stoner Produce

Oatmeal Cookies

Makes 5 dozen cookies

1¼ cups flour
1 tsp. baking soda
1 cup butter or margarine, softened
¼ cup sugar
¾ cup brown sugar
3.4-oz. pkg. instant vanilla pudding
2 eggs
3½ cups quick oats
1 cup raisins

1. Mix flour with baking soda.
2. Combine butter, sugars, and pudding mix in a large bowl. Beat until smooth and creamy.
3. Beat in eggs.
4. Gradually add flour mixture. Stir in oats and raisins. Batter should be stiff.
5. Drop by rounded teaspoonful onto ungreased cookie sheets.
6. Bake at 375° for 10-12 minutes.

—Joanne Mylin, Robert S. Meck Produce

Banana Oatmeal Cookies

Makes 4½-5 dozen cookies

1½ cups flour
1 cup sugar
½ tsp. salt
½ tsp. baking soda
½ tsp. ground cinnamon
¼ tsp. nutmeg
¾ cup butter or margarine, softened
1 egg
1 cup mashed bananas
1¾ cups cooking oats
1 cup semi-sweet chocolate chips
½ cup walnuts, chopped

1. Combine flour, sugar, salt, baking soda, cinnamon, and nutmeg in mixing bowl.
2. Cut in butter until mixture is crumbly. Stir in egg.
3. Add bananas and oats. Stir in chocolate chips and nuts.
4. Drop by teaspoonful onto ungreased cookie sheet.
5. Bake at 375° for 13-15 minutes, until golden brown. Cool.

—Mary S. King, Shreiner's Flowers

◆

Oatmeal Raisin Chews

Makes 2 1/2 dozen cookies

2 1/4 cups flour
1 tsp. baking soda
1/4 tsp. salt
1 cup quick oats (not instant)
1 cup brown sugar, packed
1/2 cup sugar
1 cup butter or margarine, softened
2 Tbsp. honey
2 tsp. vanilla
2 large eggs
1 1/2 cups (8 oz.) raisins
1/2 cup (2 oz.) walnuts, chopped, optional

1. Preheat over to 300°.
2. In a medium bowl combine flour, soda, salt, and oats. Mix well with wire whisk. Set aside.
3. In a large bowl blend sugars with electric mixer at medium speed. Add butter. Mix to form a grainy paste.
4. Scrape down sides of bowl. Add honey, vanilla, and eggs. Mix at medium speed until fully combined.
5. Add flour mixture, raisins, and walnuts. Blend at low speed until just combined. Do not over-mix.
6. Drop by teaspoonful onto ungreased cookie sheets, about 2" apart.
7. Bake for 18-22 minutes, or until cookies are light golden brown.
8. Immediately transfer cookies with a spatula to a cool, flat surface.

—Marian A. Sweigart, S. Clyde Weaver, Inc.

Market Rules 1889

• It shall be unlawful to move or push out of place any stall or stand. The number of the stall shall not be obscured, nor shall any sign be put up above or higher than said number. No additions shall be made to the stalls or stands, neither by adding nor taking away shelves or other devices. No foot boards shall be used back of the stalls; but carpets or rugs may be used to stand on; provided that they are removed at the close of the market.

Oatmeal Maple Syrup Drop Cookies

Makes 4 dozen cookies

1/2 cup shortening
1 cup maple syrup
1 egg, beaten
1 1/2 cups flour
1 tsp. salt
2 tsp. baking powder
1/2 cup milk
1/2 cup seedless raisins
1 1/2 cups oatmeal
1/2 cup nuts, chopped

1. Beat together shortening, maple syrup, and egg.
2. Sift flour, salt, and baking powder. Add this to first mixture alternately with milk. Mix well.
3. Add raisins, oatmeal, and nuts.
4. Drop by teaspoonsful onto greased cookie sheets.
5. Bake at 375° for 15 minutes.

—Elton Moshier, Pure Maple Syrup

Maple Syrup Cookies

Makes 4 dozen cookies

1 cup maple syrup
1/2 cup butter, softened
2 eggs, beaten well
1 tsp. vanilla
3 cups flour
1 tsp. baking powder
1/4 tsp. salt
1/2 cup milk

1. Cream together maple syrup and butter. Add eggs and vanilla.
2. Sift together flour, baking powder, and salt. Add this to maple syrup alternately with milk.
3. Roll dough on a lightly floured surface to 1/8" thickness. Cut into shapes with cookie cutters. Place on greased cookie sheets.
4. Bake at 400° for 10-12 minutes.

—Elton Moshier, Pure Maple Syrup

◆

Glazed Apple Cookies

Makes 4¹/₂ dozen cookies

Cookies:
¹/₂ cup shortening
1¹/₂ cups brown sugar
1 egg, beaten
1 tsp. baking soda
1 tsp. cinnamon
1 tsp. cloves
¹/₂ tsp. nutmeg
2 cups flour
¹/₃ cup milk or apple juice
1 cup apples, finely chopped
1 cup walnuts
1 cup raisins

Glaze:
1¹/₂ cups confectioners sugar
1 Tbsp. margarine, softened
¹/₂ tsp. vanilla
¹/₈ tsp. salt
2¹/₂ Tbsp. milk or sour cream
2 to 3 oz. cream cheese, softened

1. Cream ¹/₂ cup shortening and 1¹/₂ cups brown sugar together. Add egg and beat well.
2. Mix dry ingredients together (excluding fruit and nuts).
3. Add to creamed mixture alternately with milk or juice. Mix until smooth.
4. Stir in fruit and nuts.
5. Drop by teaspoonful onto greased cookie sheet.
6. Bake at 400° for 10 minutes.
7. Mix glaze ingredients. Smooth over cooled cookies.

—Katie Stoltzfus, Eisenberger's Bakery

The Northern Market was a farmers market located on the northwest corner of Queen and Walnut Streets. Built in 1872, it was the first of the large market houses. The building measured 80 feet by 240 feet and contained 250 stalls. The relatively new market building suffered a great tragedy in 1883, when the roof collapsed from the weight of snow. When the market closed in 1953, there were only 15 occupied stands. The building was demolished in 1958.

◆

Date and Nut Balls
Makes 30-40 balls

1 stick margarine
3/4 cup sugar
1/2 lb. dates, chopped fine
2 egg yolks
21/2-3 cups crispy rice cereal
1/2 cup English walnuts, chopped
1 tsp. vanilla
coconut, grated

1. Combine margarine, sugar, dates, and egg yolks. Cook over low heat for 2 minutes.
2. Remove from heat. Cool slightly.
3. Add crispy rice cereal, walnuts, and vanilla.
4. Form into small balls and roll in coconut.
5. Serve. No baking needed!

—*Joyce Denlinger, S. Clyde Weaver, Inc.*

Crunchy Peanut Cookies
Makes 3 dozen cookies

1 lb. salted peanuts, chopped
2 beaten egg whites
1 cup sugar
1 Tbsp. flour

1. Combine all ingredients. Mix well by hand.
2. Shape into balls and place on greased cookie sheet.
3. Bake at 350° for 15 minutes.
4. Allow to cool on cookie sheet before removing.

—*Marty Stauffer, S. Clyde Weaver, Inc.*

◆

Walnut Frosties

Makes 2 dozen cookies

Cookies:
1 cup brown sugar
1/2 cup butter or margarine, softened
1 egg
1 tsp. vanilla
2 1/4 cups flour
1 tsp. baking soda
1/4 tsp. salt

Topping:
1 cup walnuts, finely chopped
1/2 cup brown sugar
1/4 cup sour cream

1. Cream together sugar and butter.
2. Add egg and vanilla. Beat well.
3. Add remaining cookie ingredients and mix thoroughly.
4. Shape batter into 1" balls.
5. Mix together topping ingredients.
6. Make a depression in the center of each cookie. Place 1 tsp. topping in it.
7. Bake at 350° for 12 minutes on greased cookie sheets.

—Marian King, Shreiner's Flowers

Walnut Kisses

Makes about 3 dozen small cookies

3 egg whites
1 cup granulated sugar
pinch of cream of tartar
1 cup black walnut meats
     (don't chop finer than they are in the package)

1. Mix egg whites, sugar, and cream of tartar in small mixer bowl. Beat for 10 minutes at high speed.
2. Fold in walnuts.
3. Cover cookie sheets with waxed paper. Drop cookies by well-rounded teaspoonsful onto cookie sheets.
4. Bake on middle oven rack at 250° for 25-30 minutes.

Dorothy W. Stauffer, Nye's Sandwich Haus

English Tea Tarts
Makes 18 servings

1 cup butter, softened
2 cups flour, sifted
6 oz. cream cheese, softened
1/4 cup pecans, chopped

Filling:
2 eggs, beaten slightly
1 1/2 cups brown sugar
1/2 tsp. vanilla
2 Tbsp. butter
1/4 tsp. salt
1/2 cup pecans, chopped

1. Cream butter, flour, and cream cheese. Chill for 30 minutes.
2. Spoon dough by teaspoonful into muffin tins. Press dough with thumb to form a cup shape.
3. Sprinkle pecans into each cup.
4. Mix together filling ingredients.
5. Fill tart shells with filling mixture. Sprinkle each tart with pecans.
6. Bake at 325° for 25-30 minutes.
—*Mary Ellen Campbell, Baskets of Central Market*

Market Rules, 1889

• Sixty-six stalls, numbered from 1 to 66 inclusive, are set apart for the retailing of meats, and it shall be unlawful for anyone to retail fresh meats anywhere else within the Market limits; provided, however, that farmers who do not make a business of butchering shall have the privilege to dispose of the surplus meats, etc., after their annual butchering, at their own stall.
• Sixteen stalls, numbered 139 to 142 inclusive, and 175 to 182 inclusive, and 215 to 218 inclusive, are set apart for Bakers, for the sale of Bread, Cakes, etc., and it shall be unlawful to engage in said business anywhere else in the Market House.
• Eight stalls, numbered 67 to 70 inclusive, and 95 to 98 inclusive, are set apart for Dried Meat and Cheese Dealers, and it shall be unlawful to carry on said business anywhere else in the Market House; provided, that farmers, who do not make a business of butchering and drying meats, shall have the privilege to dispose of their surplus dried meats after their annual butchering at their own stall, and also of selling their homemade cheese.

◆

Whoopie Pies

Makes 3 dozen whoopie pies

1 cup shortening
2 cups sugar
2 eggs
1 cup baking cocoa
4 cups flour, heaped
1 tsp. salt
1 cup sour milk (or 1 cup milk with 1 Tbsp. vinegar)
2 tsp. vanilla
2 tsp. baking soda
1 cup hot water

Filling:
2 egg whites
2 tsp. vanilla
4 Tbsp. milk
2 cups confectioners sugar
1¹/2 cups shortening
2 cups confectioners sugar

1. Cream shortening and sugar together. Add eggs and blend well.
2. Stir together cocoa, flour, and salt.
3. Add milk and vanilla alternately with dry ingredients. Mix well.
4. Dissolve baking soda in hot water. Stir into batter.
5. Drop by tablespoonsful on a lightly greased cookie sheet.
6. Bake for 8 minutes at 400°. Cool.
7. To prepare whoopie pie filling, beat egg whites until soft peaks form. Fold in vanilla, milk, and 2 cups confectioners sugar.
8. Beat well. Add shortening and remaining confectioners sugar. Blend thoroughly.
9. Spread a generous amount of filling between two cookies. Wrap whoopie pies individually for a snack or dessert.

—*Barbara Finefrock, Willow Valley Farm*

Central Market is now the only farmers market in Lancaster; however, there were at least eight other markets that once operated within the city. Central Market has by far the longest history; only two other city markets lasted more than a hundred years. Three Lancaster markets endured for less than 40 years. From 1882 to 1965 there were at least five farmers markets operating simultaneously within Lancaster. The high point was between 1907 and 1918 when there were seven markets in the city.

◆

Shoe String Apple Pie
Makes 1 9" pie

3/4-1 cup white sugar
2 tsp. cornstarch
3 eggs, well beaten
1/4 cup water
4 cups apples, peeled and shredded
9" unbaked pie crust

1. Mix first 5 ingredients together. Pour into unbaked pie crust.
2. Bake at 375° for 50-60 minutes.

—*Rachel King, Shreiner's Flowers*

Sour Cream Apple Crumb Pie
Makes 1 9" pie

6 apples, pared and sliced
1/2 cup raisins
6 Tbsp. sugar
2 Tbsp. flour
1 cup sour cream
1 egg, beaten
1 tsp. vanilla
pinch of salt

Crumb topping:
1/2 cup flour
1/4 cup white sugar
1/4 cup brown sugar
1 tsp. cinnamon
sprinkle of nutmeg
1/3 cup butter or margarine, softened

9" unbaked pie crust

1. Fill unbaked pastry crust with apples and raisins.
2. In a mixing bowl, stir sugar and flour together. Fold in sour cream, beaten egg, vanilla, and salt.
3. Spoon cream mixture over apples and raisins.
4. Bake 40 minutes at 350° or until pie is golden brown.
5. To prepare crumb topping, blend flour, sugars, cinnamon, and nutmeg together. Cut in butter until mixture is crumbly.
6. Spoon crumbs over top of pie and bake 15 minutes more, or until crumbs are lightly browned.

—*Mrs. Sam Kauffman, Kauffman's Fruit Farm*

◆

Peach Supreme Pie

Makes 1 10" pie

3/4 cup flour
1 tsp. baking powder
1/2 tsp. salt
3 Tbsp. butter or margarine, softened
1 egg
1/2 cup milk
3-oz. pkg. vanilla pudding (not instant)
29-oz. can sliced peaches, or 1 qt. home-canned peaches
8 oz. cream cheese, at room temperature
1/2 cup sugar
1/2 tsp. cinnamon
1 Tbsp. sugar

1. Mix together flour, baking powder, salt, butter, egg, milk, and dry vanilla pudding. Pour into a greased 10" glass pie dish.
2. Drain peaches, reserving 3 Tbsp. peach juice. Place peaches in pie dish, keeping them about 1" from all sides of the plate.
3. Cream together cream cheese, 1/2 cup sugar, and reserved 3 Tbsp. peach juice. Cover peaches with this mixture.
4. Sprinkle pie with cinnamon and 1 Tbsp. granulated sugar. Bake at 350° for 30-35 minutes.

—*Ann White, Sunflower Foundation*

The North American, Philadelphia, Sunday, July 5, 1908

How Is This for a Housewife's Paradise?

Saturday is the big market day. From outlying towns, people come on trolley cars with great big baskets. From towns five, 10 and 15 miles away, thrifty housewives come; even from Philadelphia many come on Saturdays with great hampers, to [gather] in the week's supply of vegetables. Scores of families of railroad employees living in Philadelphia who enjoy annual passes do their marketing in Lancaster.

From 4 o'clock in the morning—before the sun illumines the narrow streets about it—until after 9 o'clock, crowds throng the market house. From 500 to 1000 persons flow in a steady stream along the aisles between the stalls at times.

Most of them are women, with big baskets holding a bushel of stuff. Some evidently are poor, with cheap dresses; others very elegantly attired.

◆

Peach Raspberry Crumb Pie
Makes 1 9" pie

3 cups ripe peaches, peeled and sliced
1 cup sugar
1 cup red raspberries
2 Tbsp. flour
1 Tbsp. tapioca

9" unbaked pie crust

Crumb Topping:
1/4 cup brown sugar
1/4 cup white sugar
3/4 cup flour
1/3 cup shortening

1. Mix together pie ingredients and pour into unbaked pie crust.
2. Mix Crumb Topping dry ingredients together.
3. Cut shortening into those ingredients. Crumble over fruit filling.
4. Bake at 425° for 10 minutes. Reduce heat to 375° and bake for 35 to 40 minutes, until pie filling bubbles.

—*Ethel Stoner, John R. Stoner Produce*

Pumpkin Custard Pie
Makes 2 8"-pies or 1 10"-pie

1 1/2 Tbsp. butter, at room temperature
1 1/2 cups sugar
3 egg yolks
1 1/2 heaping tsp. flour
1 1/2 cups cooked pumpkin
3 cups milk
3 egg whites, stiffly beaten
cinnamon, to garnish

1 or 2 unbaked pie crusts

1. Cream butter and sugar. Add egg yolks and mix well.
2. Blend flour, pumpkin, and milk. Add to creamed mixture. Fold in stiffly beaten egg whites.
3. Pour into pie crusts. Sprinkle with cinnamon.
4. Bake at 400° for 40-45 minutes.

—*Bill Cox, Minnich's Farm Bakery*

French Rhubarb Pie
Makes 1 9" pie

Filling:
3 cups rhubarb, cut in small pieces
2 eggs, beaten
1¹/₂ cups sugar
1¹/₄ -1¹/₂ tsp. vanilla
3 Tbsp. flour

9" unbaked pie crust

Crumbs:
³/₄ cup flour
¹/₂ cup brown sugar
¹/₃ cup butter, at room temperature

1. Combine filling ingredients. Stir well.
2. Pour filling into pie crust.
3. Combine dry ingredients for crumbs. Cut in butter until mixture becomes crumbly. Sprinkle on top of pie.
4. Bake at 400° for 10 minutes. Continue baking at 350° for 40 minutes, or until rhubarb is soft when pricked with a fork.
—*Yvonne Thomas Martin, Thomas Produce*

Mile High Strawberry Pie
Makes 1 10" pie

10 oz. frozen or fresh strawberries, crushed
³/₄ cup sugar
2 egg whites
1 Tbsp. lemon juice
¹/₈ tsp. salt
¹/₂ cup whipping cream, whipped
1 tsp. vanilla
10" baked pie crust

1. Place defrosted or fresh strawberries, sugar, egg whites, lemon juice, and salt in large bowl.
2. Beat on medium speed for 15 minutes, until stiff.
3. Fold in whipped cream and vanilla.
4. Pile lightly into pie crust. Freeze pie for several hours or overnight.
5. Serve pie directly from freezer.

"I like to pour crushed berries over each serving."
—*Hilda M. Funk, Givant's Jewish Baked Goods*

◆

Spring Strawberry Pie

Makes 1 9" pie

1 cup baking mix
1/4 cup butter or margarine, softened
3 Tbsp. boiling water
1 qt. fresh strawberries, washed and stemmed
1 cup sugar (or a bit less, if desired)
3 Tbsp. cornstarch
1/2 cup water
several drops red food coloring, optional
whipped cream, to garnish

1. Preheat oven to 425-450°.
2. Combine baking mix and butter. Add boiling water. Stir with fork until dough forms a ball.
3. Pat dough evenly into a 9" pie pan. Flute edges. Prick dough with a fork.
4. Bake pie crust 8-10 minutes or until slightly brown. Cool.
5. Mash enough berries to yield 1 cup.
6. Blend sugar and cornstarch. Stir in water, food coloring, and mashed berries.
7. Cook until the mixture boils, stirring constantly. Boil 1 minute, or until thickened.
8. Arrange remaining whole berries in the pie crust. Pour cooked mixture over berries.
9. Refrigerate for several hours. Serve with whipped cream.
—*Joyce Denlinger, S. Clyde Weaver, Inc.*

Cool 'n Easy Strawberry Pie

Makes 6 servings

2/3 cup boiling water
3-oz. pkg. strawberry gelatin
1/2 cup cold water
ice cubes
8 oz. whipped topping
1 cup strawberries, fresh or frozen

1 graham cracker crumb crust

1. In a large bowl, stir boiling water into gelatin for 2 minutes, or until dissolved.
2. Mix cold water and ice to make 1 1/4 cups.
3. Add ice water to gelatin, stirring slightly until thickened. Remove any remaining ice.

◆

4. Stir in whipped topping with wire whisk until smooth. Mix in fruit.
5. Refrigerate 20-30 minutes, or until mixture is very thick and mounds.
6. Spoon into crust. Refrigerate for 4 hours or until firm.

Variation: This is also good with peach gelatin and fresh peaches.
—Anne Wilson, Hodecker Celery Farm

Strawberry Cheese Pie
Makes 1 9" pie

Filling:
3-oz. pkg. strawberry gelatin
1 cup boiling water
2 cups fresh strawberries, halved and sweetened
4 oz. cream cheese
1/2 cup sugar
1½ cups whipped topping

Crust:
1½ cups graham cracker crumbs (18 crackers)
3 Tbsp. sugar
1/3 cup butter or margarine, melted

1. Combine crust ingredients. Press evenly on bottom and along sides of pie pan.
2. Bake crust at 350° for 10 minutes.
3. Dissolve gelatin in boiling water.
4. Drain berries. Measure syrup. Add water to syrup to make 1/2 cup liquid.
5. Add liquid to gelatin. Stir in strawberries. Chill until mixture begins to congeal.
6. Meanwhile, whip cream cheese until soft. Beat in sugar.
7. Blend whipped topping with cheese mixture.
8. Place cheese mixture in baked graham cracker crust, mounding at edges.
9. Spoon strawberry mixture into pie, still allowing cream cheese to show.
10. Chill until fruit is set, approximately 3 hours. Top with additional whipped topping before serving.
—Joanne Warfel, S. Clyde Weaver, Inc.

Montgomery Pie

Makes 1 9" pie

Bottom half:
1/2 cup sweet molasses
1/2 cup sugar
1 cup water
1 egg
2 Tbsp. flour
juice of one lemon
1 tsp. lemon rind, grated

Top half:
2/3 cup sugar
1/4 cup butter or shortening, softened
1 egg, beaten
1/2 cup sour milk
1 1/4 cups flour
1 1/4 tsp. baking soda

9" unbaked pie crust

1. Combine ingredients for bottom half of pie. Pour into pie crust.
2. To prepare top half of pie, beat sugar, butter, and beaten egg together.
Add milk and sifted dry ingredients alternately.
3. Spread topping over mixture in pie crust.
4. Bake at 375° for 35-40 minutes.

"You can call this pie or cake. My mother often made it to serve to field-workers at harvest time."

—Helen A. Thomas, Thomas Produce

Market Rules, 1889

• Not more than two families or the representatives of more than two separate interests will be permitted to occupy one and the same stall at one and the same time.
• Persons renting stalls shall keep the same clean.

◆

Gooseberry Pie

Makes 1 8" pie

3 cups gooseberries
1 cup brown sugar
1 cup sugar
1 Tbsp. flour
1 egg, beaten
3 Tbsp butter or margarine, melted
1/2 tsp. cloves

8" unbaked pie crust, with top crust

1 egg yolk
1 Tbsp. water
sugar

1. Mix gooseberries, sugars, flour, egg, butter, and cloves. Place in pie crust.
2. Cover pie with the top crust. Cut a few holes in the top crust to allow steam to escape.
3. Mix egg yolk and water. Paint top of pie. Sprinkle generously with sugar.
4. Bake at 450° for 15 minutes. Reduce heat to 350° and bake for 30 minutes.
—*Mabel Haverstick, Viv's Varieties*

Cheese Pie

Makes 6 servings

1 egg, beaten
8 oz. cream cheese, softened
1/3 cup sugar
1/4 tsp. vanilla
1 cup sour cream
2 Tbsp. sugar
1/4 tsp. vanilla
pinch of salt

1 graham cracker crumb crust

1. Preheat oven to 375°.
2. Mix together egg, cream cheese, 1/3 cup sugar, and 1/4 tsp. vanilla. Pour into pie crust.
3. Bake for 12 minutes. Remove from oven. Set oven temperature to 425°.
4. Mix together sour cream, 2 Tbsp. sugar, 1/4 tsp. vanilla, and salt. Pour on top of pie.
5. Bake at 425° for 2-5 minutes. Chill 24 hours.
—*Pamela Rohrer, Sensenig's Gourmet Turkey*

◆

Quakertown Pie

Makes 2 9" pies

Filling:
1 cup brown sugar
1/2 cup sweet molasses
2 cups hot water
1 egg, beaten
1 heaping Tbsp. flour
1/2 tsp. vanilla
dash of salt

Crumbs:
1 cup brown sugar
2 cups flour
1 tsp. baking powder
1/2 cup margarine, at room temperature

2 9"-unbaked pie crusts

1. Combine filling ingredients. Boil until thickened, stirring constantly.
2. Combine dry crumb ingredients. Cut in margarine until mixture is crumbly.
3. Pour cooked mixture into unbaked pie crusts.
4. Gently sprinkle crumbs on top.
5. Bake at 375° for 35 minutes.

"This recipe was handed down to me from my grandmother, who was born in the late 1800s. This pie can be served with any meal."
—*Kitty Longenecker, Givant's Jewish Baked Goods*

Market Rules, 1889

• **Hawking or Peddling within the Market House is strictly prohibited.**

Central Market Standholders

Note: If it was known that a stand was purchased at a December auction, the stand was given a founding date in the next year. Some information was obtained directly from the standholders, some came from newspaper articles, and some came from the few available official records.

Achenbach's D-11,12
since 1996
Baked goods, pastries

Areti Greek Pastries H-9
since 1992
Greek foods

The Baker's Basket F-1
since 1988
Baked goods

Baltozer's Candies
E-13,14,15,16
since 1982
Candy

Amos Barr Produce
F-8,9,10,11
since c. 1965
Fruits, vegetables

M. E. Bell, Inc. K-9,10,11
Since 1993
Meat

Benjamin E. Barr Produce
F-12, G-7,8
since 1975
Fruits, vegetables

Baskets of Central Market
E-9,10
since 1988
Baskets

The Bread Basket H-15,16
since 1992
Bread

Rudolph Breighner D-13,14
since c. 1880
Vegetables

Brenneman Farm G-9,10
since c. 1974
Fruits, vegetables

Chet's Flower Garden
G-3,4,5,6
since 1984
Flowers

Cora's Creations L-1,2,3
since 1996
Baked goods

Creative Seasonings F-5,6
since 1995
Herbs, gifts

Eisenberger's Baked Goods
H-3,4, J-3,4
since c. 1939
Baked goods

Esh's Deli B-3,4,5,6
since 1994
Deli, salads, sandwiches

Friends and Neighbors
F-17,18,19
since 1993
Gourmet coffee

German Deli K-14,15
since 1978
German specialties, meat,
cheese, candy

Givant's Jewish Baked Goods
J-1,2
since 1959
Jewish specialties

Great Harvest Bread D-9,10
since 1996
Bread

The Goodie Shop A-4,5
since 1981
Baked goods, salads

**Anna Marie Groff's Fresh Cut
Flowers** F-7
since 1964
Flowers

Rohrer M. Groff E-17,18,19
since c. 1964
Vegetables

Heckenberger Seafood Two
A-11,12,13,14
Seafood

The Herb Shop G-17,18,19
since 1994
Herbs, teas

Hodecker Celery Farm
D-15,16
since c. 1920 or before
Celery, fruit

Horn of Plenty A-6,7,8,9,10
since 1981
Fruits and vegetables

Robert P. Howry, Inc.
K-1,2,3,4
Since 1931
Meats

Kauffman's Fruit Farms
E-1,2,3,4
since c. 1939
Fruit, preserves, bulk foods

Kiefer's Meats and Cheese
A-1,2,3
since c. 1940s
Smoked meats, cheese, salads

Kim's Candies
L-9,10
since 1986
Candy, egg rolls

Lancaster Bagel Company B-15
since 1992
Bagels

Lancaster Citrus Company
B-16,17
since 1991
Citrus juices

Lancaster Gingerbread House
H-19
since 1994
Desserts

Lancaster Pasta Company
D-19
since 1996
Pasta

Long's Horseradish H-10
since 1939
Horseradish, relishes

C.Z. Martins Sons & Martin's Deli C-5,6,7,8, 9,10
since 1923
Meat, cheese, deli

Marv & Sam's Real New York Deli M-8,9
since 1993
Deli

Robert S. Meck H-11,12,13,14
since 1975
Fruit, vegetables

Ryan C. Meck J-11,12,13,14
since 1993
Fruit, vegetables

Melissa's Favorites M-5
since 1979
Nuts, dried fruits, snacks

Michael's Homestyle Breads E-5,6
since 1988
Breads, sticky buns

Minnich's Farm Bakery C-18, D-17,18
Bakery, deli

Elton Moshier's Pure Maple Syrup G-1,2
since 1995
Maple Syrup

Mumma's Pretzel Bakery F-2,3,4
since 1986
Pretzels

Nancy's Goodies M-6,7
since 1938
Baked goods, snacks

Nye's Sandwich Haus B-1,2
since 1980
Sandwiches, soft drinks

Pasta Fresca G-11,12
since 1994
Deli, pastas

Pennsylvania Dutch Gifts H-5,6
since 1984
Gifts

Pennsylvania Fudge Company M-10
since 1994
Fudge

Pennsylvania Pickle Company J-15,16
since 1995
Pickles, relishes

Plum Street Gourmet K-16,17
since 1989
Deli

Regine's Coffee C-11,12
since 1974
Coffee, dried fruits

Ric's Breads E-11,12
since 1995
Bread, baked goods

Saife's Middle Eastern Food H-17,18
since 1990
Middle Eastern food

Sensenig's Meats K-5,6,7
since 1981
Gourmet turkey meat

Shenk's Cheese Co. D-5,6,7,8
Since c. 1880
Cup cheese, ball cheese, spreads, cheesecake

Shreiner's Flowers D-1,2,3,4
since c. 1930
Flowers

Simple Gifts Farm J-17,18
since 1996
Fruit, vegetables

Clyde Slaymaker, Jr. K-12,13
since 1976
Poultry, eggs

Spring Glen Fresh Foods, Inc. C-14,15,16,17
since 1966
Salads, desserts, spreads

Stoltzfus Baked Goods B-7,8
since 1993
Baked goods

John R. Stoner Produce G-13,14,15,16
since c. 1900
Vegetables

Sunflower Foundation E-7,8, F-13,14,15,16
since 1980
Pennsylvania Dutch crafts, gifts

C. H. Thomas & Sons, Inc. C-1,2,3,4
Since 1913
Fresh beef and pork

Thomas Produce C-19,20
since 1931
Fruits and vegetables

Utz's Potato Chips J-9,10
since c. 1925
Potato chips

Viv's Varieties J-5,6,7,8
since c. 1880s
Flowers

S. Clyde Weaver, Inc. K-8, L-4,5,6,7,8
since 1929
Meat, cheese

Willow Valley Farm B-9,10,11,12,13,14
since 1945
Baked goods, poultry, barbecued chicken

Index

About the Authors

Phyllis Pellman Good is a native of Lancaster County, Pennsylvania. As a teenager she worked on Central Market and today, as a resident of Lancaster City, shops there. She edits books related to the Amish and Mennonites and is the author of a variety of cookbooks, including the top-selling *The Best of Amish Cooking*. She is the co-author of *The Central Market Cookbook, The Best of Mennonite Fellowship Meals, From Amish and Mennonite Kitchens,* and *20 Most Asked Questions About the Amish and Mennonites.*

Phyllis and her husband Merle are the parents of two daughters.

Louise Stoltzfus is also a native of Lancaster County, Pennsylvania, and lives in downtown Lancaster. She, too, has authored several books about Amish and Mennonite life, and cooking: *Amish Women: Lives and Stories* and *Favorite Recipes from Quilters.* She is the co-author of two cookbooks with Phyllis Pellman Good—*The Central Market Cookbook* and *The Best of Mennonite Fellowship Meals.* She also co-authored the *Lancaster County Cookbook.*